INFORMATION TECHNOLOGY
A Revolutionary Change

INFORMATION TECHNOLOGY
A Revolutionary Change
(In 9 Volumes)

Volume 2
(Disparities in ICT Access and Use)

Editor
RAMESH CHANDRA
Vice-Chancellor, Bundelkhand University, Jhansi (U.P.)

KALPAZ PUBLICATIONS
DELHI–110052

INFORMATION TECHNOLOGY: A REVOLUTIONARY CHANGE

(Information Technology)

Rs. 8000 (Set)
Rs. 900 (Each Volume)

ISBN: 81-7835-201-X (Set)
ISBN: 81-7835-221-4 (Vol. 2)

Published in 2003 in India by
Kalpaz Publications
C–30, Satyawati Nagar
Delhi–110052
E-mail: kalpaz@hotmail.com

Laser Typesetting at: Varsha Graphics, Delhi
Printed at: Mehra Offset Printers, New Delhi

Contents

Preface

Today, Information and Communication Technology (ICTs) disparities usually exacerbate existing disparities based on location such as urban-rural, gender, ethnicity, physical disability, age, and, especially, income level, and between 'rich' and 'poor' countries. The digital divide is not an isolated entity, but a complicated patchwork of varying levels of ICT access, basic ICT usage, and ICT applications among countries and peoples. The private sector has slowly spread technology to middle income groups, but on the whole they fail to see the developing world and underserved populations as viable markets that require targeted products. Governments often tend to the short-term demands of their constituencies, but do not provide a coherent, long-term plan for prosperity and effective ICT integration, and a legal and regulatory framework that foster ICT use.

Dealing with the digital divide is beyond the scope of any single initiative and technology is not a silver bullet for the world's problems. It is important for organizations doing community ICT projects to bring a global perspective and an entrepreneurial approach, and they must cooperate with like-minded efforts to tackle the range of problems collaboratively. There are some of the key elements necessary for integrating technology into society in an effective, sustainable way so that people can put technology to use to improve their lives. ICT disparities are usually exacerbate existing disparities based on location, gender, ethnicity, physical disability, age, and, especially, income level, and between 'rich' and 'poor' countries.

Measures of the digital divide exists in number and cost of PCs, phones, Internet hosts, Web sites, Internet users, residential/organizational/international Internet bandwidth, technical capacity, and advanced applications like e-commerce. The spread of Internet users among the world's population is much more unequal than that of the use of other ICT such as TV or telephones. The inequality of Internet usage is even bigger than the spread of GDP between the world's rich and poor countries.

National governments can play a fundamental role in creating an environment that will foster technology use and encourage national and international investment in ICT infrastructure, development, and a skilled work-force. These include telecommunications privatisation, standards setting, consumer protection, and government usage of ICT. Economic growth and social equity are both needed to bridge international and domestic digital divides. However, no consensus exists on exactly what policies are needed for either of these goals.

Editor

1

Impacts of Information and Communication Technologies (ICTs)

Information and Communication Technologies (ICTs) represent to today's world what industrial machines represented during the industrial revolution; they have revolutionized ways of working, transformed the economy, had an irreversible impact on the way people live, and have shaped a new information society. The fundamental role of ICTs in the information and knowledge society is widely recognized, as is the fact that there is unequal distribution and sharing of this technology and of access to information.

Universal access or universal service are a fundamental point of all declarations, in particular with reference to the needs of developing countries, where the information society both opens up great potential for development and poses new risks, widening disparities between and within countries. Universal service is the long-term objective of making communication facilities available to every member of society on an individual or household basis, and it is used in particular in the regulatory-legislative framework to indicate the obligation of telecommunication operators to provide their services to the entire population.

However, the objective of universal service is still far from turning into reality in developing countries, and the universal service concept has been complemented by the concept of universal access, i.e. the opportunity for everyone, at home or at work, to be within a reasonable distance of a telephone. In fact, to connect the majority of the poor, especially those living in rural and remote areas, requires innovative approaches, including a shift from individual connectivity, which has been prevalent in developed countries, to community connectivity.

Public access points are indeed the first step toward universal service, and also contribute to raising public awareness about the benefits of communication and information technology-possibly even providing opportunities to acquire computer skills and training. The necessity of universal access to information services is stated in several declarations, which stress the need to broaden access to and use of ICTs, declaring that everyone, everywhere should be enabled to participate in the global information society. The term "universal access", however, sometimes also assume social, economic and cultural connotations, encapsulating issues concerning equality of opportunities, literacy, diversity of content, and so on.

Universal access should therefore be interpreted as material and physical access to information infrastructure and services. Lack of infrastructure, according to a Statement from Developing Countries in the DOT Force, "[is] one of the major challenges developing countries have to face in their efforts to access ICTs as a tool for development". The principle of "universality" should therefore be limited to the need to develop this infrastructure. The need for universal service, several declarations mention the necessity of giving particular attention to the development of telecommunication infrastructures in rural and remote areas, where the telecommunication system is inadequate to sustain essential services-or where there is no service at all, but which are often home to a high percentage of the population.

The physical existence of infrastructures is essential but not sufficient for development of the information society: factors of gender, level of education and literacy, household income, language, race and ethnicity are all critical determinants of ICTs utilization and access within countries, whence the necessity to promote equality of opportunity to citizens, and in particular to encourage the participation of weaker categories in the use of ICTs.

Each country should also promote measures "to help people of every age, background and location and level of physical ability to access ICTs", and States should "actively involve the youth in national and regional ICT activities; ensure better gender balance in ICT use while instituting specific programmes that address the need of women particularly those aimed at rural and disenfranchised areas." The use of voice and touch screen applications that enable a greater number of people to access ICTs and the development of applications and content suited to local needs, harness the potential of information and communication technologies, enabling the population to participate in the information society.

The fundamental element for the utilization of ICTs content. Development of local content on the Internet is a means to ensure a culturally and linguistically diverse cyberspace, and this diversity is also an important part of the cultural heritage and has to be protected.

ICTs provide new channels for the expression of this diversity and for the worldwide dissemination of locally created content. Diversity of content on the Internet would enable the participation of all and ensure sustainable access, realizing the full potential of the Internet as a source of information and knowledge. Appropriate content would also benefit the utilization of ICTs for educational purposes, training and human resources development. The quality and variety of content is of "great importance to encourage more people to join online activities", and "special emphasis should be placed on the promotion of applications that are useful for various languages, such as translation, as well as development and distribution of contents that reflect local cultural or linguistic characteristics."

The Bamako Declaration acknowledged the continent's rich cultural diversity and urged that it should be reflected in cyberspace, affirming the need to "invest in African media content as well as new technologies and develop independent production." The production of local, national and regional content in native languages, and the location of that content on regional servers, can also help in rationalizing access for local and regional traffic and promoting its exchange via the most direct route. Creation of local content, with the help of the international community and the collaboration of the private sector, should therefore be given high priority.

Diversity of content, including cultural and linguistic diversity, should be promoted. The private sector should therefore develop and build information networks with abundant capacity to accommodate a wealth of information, both locally produced and that developed in other regions and nations. Communications can be a vehicle for the implementation of the principle of freedom of expression, as stated in Article 19 of the United Nations Universal Declaration of Human Rights: "Everyone has the right to freedom of opinion and expression; this right includes freedom to hold opinions without interference and to seek, receive and impart information and ideas through any media and regardless of frontiers."

Access to information and knowledge is essentially determined by connectivity, capabilities, and content. It is in these three areas that urgent action is required to ensure full access to ICTs for developing countries. Furthermore, unless connectivity and access are affordable, reliable and secure, prospects for development of the knowledge economy are dim. Where necessary, and particularly in developing countries, physically building up the infrastructure to access to the global information society is the first step. This is then followed by optimizing the use of the information and communication infrastructure through convergence of technologies, interconnection among different networks, standardization and management of scarce resources.

Lack of infrastructure and connectivity are still the biggest challenges to the development of the information society in most developing countries. Very often, infrastructures fail to meet local demand and cannot guarantee a reliable access to global communication networks, therefore, immediate steps have to be taken "for the development of the basic infrastructure necessary for connectivity including for most remote areas." The Tokyo Declaration affirms the urgent need "to develop the necessary infrastructure that will provide access to such resources as the Internet" with the encouragement and support of government and international community, where appropriate.

The promotion of the development of state-of-the-art national and regional communication infrastructures will lead to "upgrading the "capillarity" of information and communications networks within their various territorial units, substantially upgrading key functions such as applicability and interoperability, and facilitating a swifter diffusion of technological innovations". The utilization of the optimal mix of technologies is considered a key element for the deployment of the information society. Asia-Pacific countries affirm that, in order to effectively promote the balanced development of information and communication infrastructure, taking into consideration the geographic and economic diversities of Asia-Pacific countries, it is necessary to use "different technologies and equipment according to local conditions, as well as to take account of changes such as technological convergence."

Convergence is opening up new perspectives for the ICT sector, offering opportunities for e-learning, e-commerce, e-government, e-health, environmental protection, post-war reconstruction and many other applications which are highly beneficial for social cultural and economic development. Owing to the tremendous and multiple impacts on nations and individuals, there is growing attention to multimedia convergence, and more recent declarations are taking this into account in the definition of new telecommunication regulations and development strategies.

Technological convergence is also leading to greater optimization of costs, thus leaving scope for cost reduction and resulting in greater network access. The convergence of communication and computing technologies, especially through the Internet, is the most significant feature of this information technology revolution. The Internet is a widespread information infrastructure. It is at once a worldwide broadcasting system, a mechanism for information dissemination, a medium for interaction between individuals, and a marketplace for goods and services.

It is therefore rapidly becoming a global communications and information tool and a source of considerable economic potential for individuals, firms and countries. For the efficient development of the information and communication infrastructure, harmonization and cooperation is also necessary in such fields as interconnection, standardization or management of radio frequencies.

Interconnectivity is a fundamental tool for the achievement of universal access to services, and for the growth of the information society. "Optimum conditions" should be created for interconnectivity and interoperability. The G7 States, in the conclusion of the Brussels meeting in 1995, affirmed their commitment to pursue the interconnectivity of networks and the interoperability of services through the promotion of a consensual standardisation process which is market-led and which encourages open interfaces. Standardization is another essential ingredient in extending the global reach of telecommunications: accelerating the standardisation process conducted by international bodies will contribute to developing timely and market-responsive standards.

While the standardization process is 'international' in nature, the role of the private sector is always prominent: the G7 affirmed that [c]ooperation amongst all actors should be built on private sector-led dialogue aimed at identifying critical interfaces. Telecommunication services are also based on the utilization of radio frequencies, which are a scarce resource, the allocation of which is carried out by ITU Members at the international and regional levels and by national administrations, through a licensing procedure, at the national level. For a fair and effective allocation of these resources, transparent criteria must be applied.

International cooperation and harmonization, under the auspices of ITU, should be pursued, in particular for services such as international mobile services and the implementation of global mobile and personal systems. International co-operation is essential in such fields as standardization or management of radio frequencies that are needed for cost-effective and efficient development of Information and communication infrastructure.

To improve ICT infrastructure in African countries, the Bamako Declaration, also mentions the need to establish public access points and called for the creation of an African backbone using innovative communication infrastructures, to rationalize access to the Internet. Probably today the global community is ready for a further step in the definition of ICTs development principles and strategies.

Universal access is of course the basic issue, but afterward it will be necessary an effective development of networks, and an efficient use of resources and new technologies. Secure and clearly-established conditions for the use of these technologies must also be ensured for users and operators alike. An enabling regulatory environment, a favourable investment climate and cooperation and funding of the international community are fundamental elements for the overall development of the information society. However, some basic requirements for the development of ICTs have emerged. These include:

— appropriate policy adapted to the new demands of the information society, and transparent and non-discriminatory regulation, to favour investment in telecommunication technology, mobilization of new resources and participation of private enterprises in ICT development;

— cooperation, at international, regional and national levels, coordination of efforts, exchange of information, transfer of technology and knowledge and sharing of experiences and best practices.

In the ECOSOC Ministerial Declaration the need for "a conducive environment" at a national level is considered essential for the "rapid diffusion, development and use of information technology". Similarly, ESCAP points out the necessity of a "supportive policy environment, including telecommunications policy and cyber laws" as one of the fundamental parameters for e-readiness.

The private sector "should be the driving force behind the information society" and "has a vital role to play" in investment in the development of information and communication infrastructure. For this reason, governments should work to create an environment that allows and encourages private-sector participation, for instance by establishing transparent legal frameworks. The private sector plays a leading role in the development of information and communication networks in the information society. But it is up to governments to create a predictable, transparent and non-discriminatory policy and regulatory environment necessary for the information society. Sector reforms are among the major forces shaping the development of telecommunications, and lead to greater private sector participation and competition.

This new trade and regulatory environment places even greater pressure on policy-makers, regulators and operators to acquire the necessary skills and resources to manage the evolving ICT environment. The new model of telecommunication investment, and the entry of new players onto the scene, gives rise to the need for new and "creative models of partnerships between government, the private sector and NGOs.

While the private sector may be the driving force behind the growth of the information society, governments and organizations should not forget that private initiative is market driven, which does not necessarily cater for the needs of the whole population, particularly in developing and least developed countries. In such cases, it is essential for governments to take the lead in promoting equitable participation of the whole population in the information society. However, given the high cost of this participation, individual governments of developing countries find it difficult to carry this objective without international support.

In the establishment of an enabling environment for the development of the information society, the necessity of international cooperation and of "regional and global pooling of resources" is affirmed, in particular with reference to the growing digital divide between developed and less developed countries and to the necessity to foster universal access. Efforts to bridge the digital divide, as in our societies, crucially depend on effective collaboration among all stakeholders.

Bilateral and multilateral assistance will continue to play a significant role in building the framework conditions for IT development. International cooperation should focus on the major impediments to the participation in the ICT revolution, such as lack of infrastructure, education and connectivity. Concerted actions at the national, regional and international levels are imperative for bridging the digital divide and global regional and national financing and investment institutions are urged to attach high priority to the growth of telecommunications, particularly in developing countries.

International cooperation is mostly directed at supporting and financing the development of ICTs in less industrialized countries, but also at promoting "greater international dialogue to bring together the 'best practices in the field of ICTs. Cooperation mechanisms touch every aspect of the information society, and can be applied, where appropriate, to the dialogue, awareness campaigns, the definition of appropriate policies, the development and interconnection of information infrastructures, the provision of training, the distribution of applications and the development of their contents. Exchange of information and experience are among the main objectives of regional coordination, which is focused on tackling public policies on the information society and enabling the "sharing of experience among countries in the region on preparing for the digital era.

The international community is called upon to contribute to the development of the information society by providing "technical and financial cooperation. Cooperation in an era governed by technology must involve not only financing or exchange of information and best practices, but also the transfer of technology and knowledge, in particular in favour of developing countries. [Collaborative] efforts should include transfer of technology to developing countries on a concessional and preferential terms, as mutually agreed, especially technology related to knowledge-based sectors.

Technology transfer programmes and technical cooperation are defined by the ISAD as a key policy issue and are considered fundamental also at a regional level, to harness intraregional competencies to facilitate the transition of member countries into networked societies and economies. Cooperation is essential to develop a harmonious and equitable information society, the benefits of which are truly global. The utilization of ICTs to generate, process and transmit data and information is creating new legal dilemmas, resulting in the need to reform legal protection mechanisms for users and operators.

There is a different perception of intellectual property (IP) in the digital era and new technologies are challenging the traditional instruments of protection of IP. Therefore new approaches are needed to fight violations and guarantee the adequate reward to creativity. Protection of intellectual property rights for IT-related technology is vital to promoting IT-related innovations, competition and diffusion of new technology. With the advent of e-commerce, and of online transactions, the protection of privacy and the security of personal data, from credit card numbers to home addresses or reserved information, is at stake.

Protecting privacy and personal data alongside the safeguarding of plurality of opinion play an essential role in maintaining citizens' confidence in the information society and thereby encourage user participation and strengthen competition and market access. Misuse of personal data and the circulation of indecent information, are serious threats to the stability of ICT-based economies", therefore the definition of a new regulatory system "to minimize the risks and uncertainties of the new environment generated by the information and communication technologies" is sought, to "ensure and lead to the swift expansion of electronic commerce protecting the privacy and other interests of users, consumers and small-scale producers that engage in electronic commerce.

Information security is effectively guaranteed will individuals or organisations take full advantage of information infrastructure. Citizens and society should be protected against criminal abuse of the developing networks. To protect data, however, it is not always enough to ensure the correct functioning of communication networks: cyber crimes such as hacking or the spread of computer viruses could undermine public trust in network resources. Countries should therefore cooperate in sharing information and in coordinating their efforts to prevent these crimes and to ensure network security.

ICTs in Education

Investment in basic literacy and ICT education remains the fundamental way of increasing human capacity in developing countries and should be part of every national information technology strategy. Without the knowledge and skills required to use ICTs, the use of new communication technologies will be impossible, therefore information literacy, i.e. basic skills in acquiring, managing and communicating information is essential to familiarize people with new technologies, and their use. Human resources training, in particular for teachers and students, will also increase demand for the use and application of information and technology and promote content and infrastructure growth, thus facilitating the development of the ICT service industry, in particular in developing countries.

Investment in education, research and human capacity is seen by African countries as an essential element to reverse Africa's marginalization, and could enable the continent to address its scientific and public policy challenges. The Brussels Declaration affirms the need to pursue adequate information technology education and training, which should be integrated into the regular school system, and ISAD adds the necessity of lifelong learning. In addition to the need for training in their use, ICTs can also help in promoting learning: to participate in the knowledge based economy requires new skills, openness and creativity, acquired through life-long training.

Whence the necessity to provide citizens with the tools to learn in an information society, by means of advanced multimedia information services, which can meet such requirements whilst complementing and enriching traditional education and training systems. For the rapid development of the information society, ESCAP points to the necessity of training for trainers. Along the same lines, to promote awareness of ICT issues, many South American countries given a high priority to the necessity of ICT training for political and community leaders.

The use of ICTs can enhance a large number of applications: from electronic commerce and valorization of small and medium-sized enterprises to the empowerment of small communities and groups, they can help in the promotion of good governance and decentralization, the observance of human rights, allow long-distance education and telemedicine, and help in the environmental management and monitoring.

In other words it can help the creation of a balanced and efficient society, based on the free flow and free access to information. In order to allow ICT to provide the benefits of speedier and more efficient economic and social interaction, it is essential to develop various applications. There is general agreement on the potential of ICT applications to help reduce poverty, foster sustainable development, improve health, education and skills, facilitate new and transparent governance mechanisms and reinforce popular participation and informed decision-making. ICT represents a tremendous opportunity for emerging and developing economies.

Countries that succeed in harnessing its potential can look forward to leapfrogging conventional obstacles of infrastructural development, to meeting more effectively their vital development goals, such as poverty reduction, health, sanitation, and education, and to benefiting from the rapid growth of global e-commerce. Some developing countries have already made significant progress in these areas.

The international community recognizes the need to support the development of such applications in developing countries through the mobilization of the necessary resources, cooperation, exchange of information, transfer of technologies as well as new initiatives and projects. Public authorities have an important catalytic role to play in the promotion of research, applications and generic services. They can also further initiatives in the development of applications in areas of common public interest.

Development of E-commerce

ICTs have allowed the creation of a global marketplace, and in particular have enabled small and medium-sized enterprises (SME) to participate, giving rise to good prospects of economic growth and development through electronic trade, investment and commerce. ICTs are now offering SME new opportunities for investment "to compete in the global marketplace and to have access to new business opportunities. Financing and means of promoting SME innovation and modernization need to be sought, special programmes should be undertaken and measures aiming to offer support and incentive to small to medium enterprises to get online and to use the Internet effectively will also be pursued.

Europe needs to accelerate the growth of e-commerce, especially for SMEs, so that they can consider the whole European market as their market. This requires a reliable Internal Market legal framework, which provides legal security, removes barriers to cross-border services, encourages on-line innovation and consumer trust. One of the main socially relevant areas to be targeted for the development of cost-effective and integrated solution based on ICTs is education.

Education and training are a prerequisite to the use of new information and communication technologies, but they can also help in the achievement and reinforcement of educational goals, thanks to their flexibility and their potential for interactivity.

The innovative approaches to education allowed by the advent of ICTs are highlighted in the Florianopolis Declaration, which sees distance learning, non-formal education and teacher training as an essential basis for enabling the population to play a positive role in new forms of knowledge-based production, while also promoting the access and use of information and communications technologies in methodologies designed to accelerate the educational processes of marginalized population groups and those living in extreme poverty. Human resource development is essential for sustainable social and economic prosperity, and activities that use ICT itself, such as distance learning, can be of great help in human resource development.

ICT in Health

The health sector has become one of the major users and promoters of the use of ICT tools to gather and disseminate knowledge. ICTs give professionals and researchers access to rapid exchange of information, distance learning, and access to diagnostic assistance, and in the view of many countries should be part of national health care reforms and strategies. African countries have underlined the capacity of ICTs to enhance regional approaches to major social issues, as the struggle against HIV/AIDS, and the G7 Heads of State consider "global health care applications" to be one of the main areas of concern, re-affirming the great potential of the application of telematics technologies in the field of telemedicine to fight against the major health scourges.

ICT and Administration

The use of ICTs as a tool for governance can help to foster democracy, efficiency and transparency, and may lead to an increased possibility for countries to attract foreign investment and financial assistance. As stated during the Palermo conference on e-Government for development, ICTs have the potential to dramatically broaden political participation, to increase access to information about the ways in which governments operate, and in facilitating knowledge acquisition and utilization. [...] they are as much about enhancing public administration as about improving the ways in which a society governs itself" The administrative use of ICT particularly through e-government and e-commerce to help improve the efficiency of business and public services including in rural areas.

E-government initiatives should be undertaken in the framework of broad government reform and of an enabling environment, in which connectivity and capacity constitute basic elements. The United Nation Millennium Declaration stressed the importance of ICTs to help achieving the much broader goals of the Millennium Declaration, and affirmed the need to ensure that the benefits of new technologies, especially information and communication technologies, are available to all. Digital technology is also a vital component for environmental information assessment and for early warning mechanisms.

As the World Meteorological Organization (WMO) recently commented, a universal and equitable access to meteorological, hydrological and related information is essential for the mitigation of dangerous weather' related phenomena. Access to climatological information also affects social and economic development, and is of crucial importance for the sustainable development of less industrialized countries. The diffusion and application of ICTs will also have a major impact on global employment. Telework (or e-Work) allows companies to source work independently of location, and offers to countries (industrialized or developing) that have adequate infrastructure and skills the benefits of participation in the new global economy.

It can also decrease the need for migration in urban areas. Telework, however, could have negative effects as it may contribute to the digital divide as well as to the establishment of new laws and regulations for the protection of online workers. In short, the information society is growing, and has to be open to new opportunities for the improvement of human life.

Global Information Society (GIS)

The world is in the throes of a new and highly potent revolution. This revolution will forever change the way we live, work, play, organise our societies and ultimately define ourselves. Unlike previous technological resolutions which were focused on energy and matter, this fundamental change involves our understanding of time, space, distance and knowledge. This revolution is leading to the creation of the Global Information Society (GIS).

In February 1995, Ministers from the Group of Seven Highly Industrialised Nations (G-7) and Members of the European Commission (EC) met in Brussels at the G-7 Ministerial Conference on the Information Society. This Conference re-emphasised the need for all countries, including developing countries and countries in transition. to be integrated in the GIS. However the challenges of integrating the less industrialised countries of the world into the GIS are tremendous.

As South African Executive President Thabo Mbeki argued in his keynote address to the G-7 Information Society, Conference, "there are more telephone lines in Manhattan than in all of sub-Saharan Africa" and that "half of humanity has never made a telephone call." Mbeki challenged the G-7 and the EC to convene a follow-up conference bringing together a cross-section of the developing world with the G-7 and the EU to exchange on such questions as strategy, finance and international coordination in confronting the global information and communication challenge. He offered South Africa as host for such an initiative. The Information Society and Development (ISAD) Conference is the result of that challenge.

The ISAD Conference, held in Midrand, South Africa under the auspices of South African Executive Deputy President Thabo Mbeki, included representatives from 40 countries and 18 international organisations. Delegations consisted of government ministers and senior officials, CEOs and other private sector participants, and civil society representatives. This historic conference accomplished its three primary objectives of:

— Launching, a dialogue between the developed and developing worlds and within the developing world on the emerging Global Information Society;

— Initiating the process to define a shared vision for the Global Information Society between the relevant societal sectors in the developed and developing countries.

— Working towards "Common Principles" and Collaborative Actions" to strengthen our shared vision and meet the challenges of the Global Information Society.

While we speak of a "global" information society, the Present reality is daunting. The technological gap between the less developed and industrialised countries of the world is widening. This situation must be addressed by the world community if we are to build a Global Information Society. In respect to the present reality, we acknowledge the following:

— Information and Communication Technologies and Services Have the potential to offer a significant contribution towards the promotion of sustainable growth in all countries.

— There currently exists a huge gap between the highly-industrialised countries and the less-industrialised countries in terms of information infrastructure;

— Through developing an information infrastructure and effectively utilising information and communications technologies and services, developing countries can narrow the current gap in economic and social development and prevent it from widening;

— There are tremendous and diverse needs in the developing world ,which often differ from the need of the more industrialised countries; and,

— Developing countries must assess their own requirements and strategies for entry into the Global Information Society based on their specific realities.

There is clearly an unsatisfactory level of investment in information infrastructure development in the less industrialised countries. Being able to mobilise the necessary investment, particularly from the private sector is of paramount importance to the developing countries. Of equal importance, is being able to develop networks which enable the whole of their populations to gain access to the global information infrastructure and participate in the GIS at affordable prices. In respect to mobilising the required investments for information infrastructure development, we acknowledge the following:

— There is currently an insufficient investment in developing information infrastructures in the less industrialised countries;

— There is an extensive demand for information and communications technologies and services in the developing world; and,

— To create a truly Global Information Society, we must mobilise appropriate investment.

The new techno-economic paradigm of the global economy is increasingly driven by knowledge-intensive sectors which utilise information and communications technologies. These economic sectors could form the basis of entirely new multi-media industries, products and services which could contribute to attracting investment and creating employment within national economies. In respect to employment, labour market and work in the GIS, we acknowledge the following:

— A new knowledge intensive global economy is emerging

— The new global economy can stimulate new industries and employment opportunities.

— We must attempt to minimize the risk and enhance the opportunities for Labour; and.

— Access to training and lifelong learning must be promoted.

Meeting basic needs, developing human resources, growing the economy, creating a culture of effective delivery of public services, promoting a participatory democracy and conveying different cultures and ideas are challenges jointly faced by all countries in the world. New information and communication technologies, affordable as their costs continue to fall, could help developing nations "leapfrog' entire stages of development in setting up their own information infrastructures and applications. In respect to using the potential of information technologies, we acknowledge the following:

— Information technologies have tremendous potential to: meet basic needs, develop human resources, grow economics facilitate

— new competitive advantages, improve the efficiency of government management and delivery of public services, promoting

— participatory democracy as well as cultural and linguistic diversity in each country;

— To achieve these benefits, the particular environment in each nation must be considered to promote the optimal mix of technologies in deploying the information Infrastructure; and,

— These new information and communication technologies will help developing nations "leapfrog" entire stages of development.

Key opportunities exist in the following areas:

— Enhanced capacity for the development of human resources skills and competencies;

— Improved debt management within each country;

— Improved effectiveness. efficiency and productivity in the workplace;

— Greater decision-making capability through timely access to information.

— Efficient delivery of public services through improved mechanisms and greater customer responsiveness;

— Increased access to public information;

— More efficient interface between the public and private sectors;

— Economic growth and development through electronic trade, investment and commerce, particularly for Small, Medium and

— Micro Enterprises (Smes);

— Decrease in the need for migration to urban areas.,

— Health care improvement;

— Better management of natural resources and the environment, and,

— Early warning systems for weather and other environmental phenomena.

The establishment of an advanced information and communications infrastructure requires a favorable investment climate. In many countries, achieving such an environment might necessitate changes in the regulatory framework and economic restructuring aimed at a more liberalised telecommunications sector, which could provide more choice, higher quality and better access. In attracting direct investment, national regulatory policy objectives need to be transparent and consistently applied. In respect to mobilising investment through appropriate regulatory conditions, we acknowledge the following:

— In order to mobilise and attract investment, developing countries must create a climate conductive to investment;

— This necessitates an adaptable regulatory framework based upon competition and aiming at the provision of more choice, higher quality and better access;

— The process should take into account the particular realities in each country and,

— Investment in indigenous content creation should be encouraged.

The information society has the potential to enhance the quality of life of all participants. However, the scale pace of improvements in social welfare and economic development will depend heavily on the universal enabling environment. The social and societal benefits of the information infrastructure will be optimised by an approach which aims at the highest possible levels of participation. The alternative would lead to the emergence of two "information-classes" of citizens. In the developing world, the risk of creating a two-tiered society, where only one group of the population has access to new network services, and equipment, is even greater than in the developed countries. In respect to social and societal aspect of the GIS, we acknowledge the following:

— The Information Society must enhance the quality of life for all participants and avoid developing a two-tiered society;

— Life-long Education is a major key to enable full and active participation by all citizens in the GIS; and,

— Indigenous content creation should address the cultural and linguistic requirements of each

The potential rewards of working together towards a GIS are enticing and include: a better balance in economic and social progress between nations, growth of the global economy; the capacity to solve common societal problems, enhancing the progress of democratic values, and sharing as well as augmenting cultural creativity, traditions and identities. On this shared vision of human enrichment, we acknowledge the following:

— A consensus is emerging about the importance of global information society;

— No single, model is universal; and,

— A globally cooperative approach is required.

Like all societies, the GIS needs to be built on a set of common norms, on tolerance, on respect of diversity and on habits of collaboration and combined efforts. Easing its birth like dealing with all major "shifts", means overcoming uncertainties and a break in continuity. While it is bringing our world closer together, existing differences in social and economic development are becoming more apparent and the difficulties they create are worsening. In respect to launching a dialogue between the developed and developing world we acknowledge the following:

— Building the GIS requires common guidelines, tolerance, respect for diversity and collaborating actions; and,

— Distinct national visions should converge into a shared global vision.

— Encourage further discussions towards identifying and implementing Global Information Society Projects in conjunction with non-governmental organisations and international organisations;

— Share information on best practices of development programmes and usage of information and communication technologies;

— Call upon international organisations to re-assess and refocus their development tools to give active follow-up to the principles and policies identified at this conference; and

— Fully utilise various policies and private and public financial instruments available for the development of the Global Information Society

Participants welcomed the contribution of representatives of civil society and business leaders in the proceedings of the Conference. They re-emphasised the need of public and private sector co-operation and partnership in achieving common goals. These ISAD conclusions are informed by a commitment to ensure that the development of the Global Information Society benefits all humanity

The developing and developed worlds should. agree on the principles for cooperation in the GIS. Close collaboration at the highest level will ensure the efficient introduction and development of a truly "Global" information society and prevent the marginalization of some countries from this inevitable revolution. Like all societies, the Global Information Society needs to be built on a set of principles, on respect of diversity and on collaboration.

Following the principles endorsed by the Brussels conference which are:

- promoting dynamic competition
- encouraging private investment
- defining an adaptable regulatory framework
- providing open access to networks while
- ensuring universal provision of and access to services
- promoting equality of opportunity to the citizen
- promoting diversity of content, including cultural and linguistic diversity
- recognising the necessity of worldwide co-operation with particular attention to less developed countries and taking into account the key policy issues identified at the ISAD conference, which are:
  a) universal service
  b) clear regulatory framework
  c) sustainable socio-economic development
  d) employment creation
  e) global co-operation and competitiveness
  f) diversity of applications and content
  g) diversity of language and culture
  h) co-operation in technology.
  i) private investment and competition

j) protection of intellectual property rights

k) privacy and data security

l) narrowing the infrastructure gap

m) co-operation in research and technological development

n) the ISAD participants are therefore resolved to continuing the dialogue and taking appropriate action on these principles and policy issues.

Furthermore we are committed to:

— Fostering partnerships between the public and private sectors;

— Continue or begin a process of national information society planning in each of our countries which is ultimately in concert with the development of a Global Information Society;

— Encourage further discussion towards identifying and implementing Global Information Society Projects in conjunction With non-governmental organisation;

— Share information on best practices of development programmes and usage of information and communication technologies;

— Call upon international organisations to re-asses and refocus their development tools to give active follow-up to the principles and policies identified at this conference; and,

— Fully utilise various policies and private and public financial instruments available for the development of Global Information Society

Participants welcomed the contribution or representatives of civil society and business leaders in the proceedings of the Conference. They re-emphasised the need of public and private sector co-operation and partnership in achieving common goals. These ISAD conclusions are informed by a commitment to ensure that the development of the Global Information Society benefits all humanity.

Social and Ethical Impacts of ICT Applications

The social and ethical implications of ICTs warrant special attention and have resulted in the creation of a discrete area of research that has attracted people from sociology, philosophy, law, psychology as well as computer science and information systems.

In the information age, people are working in a location independent manner. This means we need to think about why direct interaction is advantageous. Interaction with others gives the possibilities and advantages of friendship. Yet, traditionally, friendship has needed face-to-face interaction.This 'virtual friendship' gives rise to problems for workers:

— *Creativity:* it is easier to explore apparently wild ideas face-to-face, in private and unmonitored. Many ideas eventually implemented start life as debates about 'wild' ideas

— *Isolation:* even the most advanced communications technologies cannot prevent feelings of isolation. Remote workers may also either be forgotten or fear they will be forgotten

— *Personal Development:* much personal development takes place informally at work. For many this can be one of the great benefits of working life. A high proportion of informal contact is lost if communication is down-the-wire.

The Location independent working (LIW) can affect:

— Capacity for the employer/manager/ supervisor to manage work: management by results moves to the forefront, when it might not have been considered for location dependent working

— Capacity for employees to negotiate conditions (partly because union organisation is more difficult among isolated workers)

— Trust and privacy, if electronic surveillance techniques are used.

— Location Independent: Working radically affects the relationship between work and the community. Much of our world is structured around there being set places of work: whole service industries survive on providing for workers in those workplaces.

Similarly, LIW can radically affect the home and the community around the home. Virtually all LIW involves either work at home or work much closer to home. Greater presence in the home community in daytime means more trade for local shops. Less time spent travelling means more time for involvement in community activities. Reductions in travel associated with work can also be expected to reduce pollution and road congestion where LIW is introduced. When some work is within the house, it takes up space that could be used for household activities.

The information age can be expected to have substantial effects on work. There is increasing globalisation of work. Some industries are 'geographically footloose'. These industries are increasingly using ICTs to redistribute work around the globe. This looks likely to involve the retention of the most sophisticated and high value roles in what are currently the most economically dominant regions of industrialised countries, while less economically rewarding roles are 'exported'. This might lead to increases in levels of incomes in the countries and regions that receive the 'exported' employment. At the same time, global inequality may still increase further. Work is increasingly becoming knowledge-and skills-based. Those without the knowledge and skills, and without the means of obtaining them, are increasingly being excluded from well-paid work.

This exclusion is amplified if they are also excluded from access to advanced information and communications technologies, whether in less industrialised countries or areas of deprivation in more industrialised countries. Increasing numbers of workers are suffering repetitive strain injuries (RSI) from over-intensive use of keyboards, and use of ergonomically poor workplaces. Technologies that might reduce the use of keyboards also appear to give rise to RSIs, so there is little cause for optimism Often this can be an intrusion. When the house is small the intrusion will be greater: meaning that this intrusion will be greater for less wealthy workers. Beyond this, there is the psychological intrusion of work on the home. A lack of physical distance can cause a lack of emotional distance: work in the home can make it impossible to get away from work. Equally, someone calling at the door of the house on personal business may interrupt work for someone working at home: whereas if they are at work in a traditional workplace, the caller is inevitably ignored. Where a traditional workplace has a culture of long hours, and the team also includes some working at home, those working at the traditional workplace have been known to call those working at home 'teleshirkers'. Colleagues working in a more traditional way can easily resent the flexibility offered to LIWorkers. Changing work patterns can also be expected to have effects on the design of offices and homes. More homes are likely to be built with one or two offices as part of the design. Meanwhile, if people are spending less time in traditional workplaces, it is to be expected that less space will be needed by these traditional workplaces. This can mean cost savings for employers. Perhaps some of the space no longer needed for offices will be taken over by housing, although the evidence seems to suggest that this will be largely by new employment using less offices while the more-or-less normal turnover of posts reduces the number intensively using offices in the traditional way.

ICTs bring ever more data to the desk of many workers. Information overload can be a severe problem, leading to excessive stress. Technology is enabling more employers to consider the use of surveillance. This 'threatens to undermine the autonomy and dignity of workers'. This can lead to a breakdown of trust between the employer and employee, to the detriment of both.

The advent of the digital age and the information society has increased the opportunities to collect and store information. Traditionally organisations kept information on personnel, products and payroll. Now information is collected on, for example, the buying habits of the supermarket shopper or the on-line behaviour of a bank's internet customers. There is often little clarity either within or outside the organisation about how the data will help the organisation's business, who should access it, or, indeed, whether the information becomes a commodity in its own right to be sold on.

As the Internet appears to have the effect of speeding up our world there is more concern about the products of endeavours rather than the manner in which these endeavours are undertaken. Product rather than process becomes all. An inclusive perspective on planning, designing and implementing information systems with a wider rather than a narrower horizon. Study of information system where the perception of what and whom should be considered was narrow. All the stakeholders were internal to the organisations and in close proximity to the projects.

There is a much wider range of potential stakeholders in any information system development that wishes to achieve a socially and ethically sensitive outcome. Included among such stakeholders would be owners, employees, unions, capital providers, government, customers, suppliers, community groups and competitors. If all the relevant stakeholders are taken on board at the outset of a project the process will embrace 'the views and concerns of all parties affected by the project.' Concerns over, for example, deskilling of jobs and redundancy effect the whole community relating to the enterprise.

The need to move away from the 'supplier-centric' model of information systems. A user-centric view with cultural, behavioural and social issues being addressed. A user-centric view recognises that information arises at the point of understanding rather than from the point of provision.

The use of information involves making judgements as to the relevance of the information, its value and its potential effect on the actions of the individual and the organisation. Thus information may be labelled as valuable or worthless, as company confidential or non-confidential, as private or public, by both the individual and the organisation. Such interpretations will determine what information is gathered, how it is searched for, how it is arranged and what use it is put to. The meaning placed on the information is influenced by the attitudes and values of the individual and the organisation. An individual's attitudes and values are informed by their cultural, religious, political and economic circumstances. These may, or may not, match the purpose of the organisation and the often unwritten culture of the organisation they work within.

Ethical use of information highlights issues of:

— privacy and confidentiality
— ownership and accessibility
— equity
— accuracy
— quality and reliability.

The issues above may equally be adequately addressed by an organisation running a website selling pornography as by a social services department dealing with sensitive personal information. A web business may well assure its customers of privacy and confidentiality, quality and reliability. The crucial issue of individual privacy and the need to manage the use of personal information in a way that balances the needs of all parties in an acceptable manner. The difficulties of identifying 'all parties' and the fact that their needs or interests may not be determined in a straightforward manner.

The concept of 'balance of interest' is flawed, both as an outcome and a process and that "ultimately it is a political process involving conflict as well as consensus involving data controlling organisations, individuals, regulatory organisations, judicial and political bodies, and others." This idea is supported by Whittington who sees problems balancing the needs of different stakeholders even within an organisation "where there are conflicting drivers and issues of security against availability".

Increasingly the balancing act has to take on the complexity of crossing national boundaries, including different legal entities, cultures and norms. Ethical codes are increasingly having an impact on information provision. Ever more professionals dealing with the information systems are members of bodies with codes.

For ethical outcomes there is a need for integrity, moral attitudes and judgements. Many in the criminal fraternity operate under a self-regulated and strictly enforced code of conduct. One would be unlikely to conclude that the mafia, for example, was an ethical organisation in consequence.

The challenge for socially responsible information provision is therefore multiplied. This is because what are addressing is:

— the need and means of educating information system developers who are able to integrate the ethical dimension into their work, and

— the need to develop a society where the norm is for organisations and businesses to behave ethically, morally and with integrity in all their transactions.

Occupations in information and communications technology may require detailed knowledge, and there may be internally defined codes of conduct for some; but they don't have closed memberships, or professional bodies with meaningful sanction powers. One of the factors that has long marked out the professions in the minds of the public is that members of the public accept that they do not themselves have specialist knowledge and they therefore trust the better judgement of professionals in these areas. True professionals are those that respect this trust, and earn and deserve it, by looking beyond their own narrow self-interest and the self-interest of their employers.

Professionalism and excellence require much more than delivering on time and within budget. There are occasions when to deliver what is requested on time and within budget would mean to deliver a dangerous and/ or malfunctioning system.

Ethical awareness should be part of the job specification for jobs in ICT; this could be tested at interview — however: there could well be practical difficulties finding candidates who would meet this criterion, at least in the short term. If cannot recruit ethically sensitive staff: in-house ethics education sessions should be run. These should not be just a one-off session at induction, but an approach that encourages continuous staff development and on-going discussion of ethical issues There are doubts about whether staff could be trained into an organisation's value system when they may already have developed a value system of their own; however there is evidence that ethical training can be effective. Impartiality is impossible: the aim should be to help staff recognise this and to become aware of their own biases.

In many organisations, the IS community is quite separate from the rest of the organisation; it would be themselves and publicise what they are doing. IS departments should be open to outside scrutiny and audit. The boundaries of responsibility for each job need to be clear. Nonetheless, it is important to avoid a narrow task focus. The aim should be towards a more holistic view of responsibilities: to all stakeholders.

— Responsibilities don't stop at the doors of the company: responsibilities are wider than to personnel within the company.

— Standards for ethical behaviour should be specified and evaluation of employees' performance against them should be included in their annual appraisal, with direct links to salary and/or promotion prospects.

— The Individual Professional and the Wider Profession Because there is a moral responsibility on professionals to look beyond their narrow self-interest, there are a range of obligations in the way they interrelate to the wider profession.

— New recruits to the profession will look around them to see what behaviour is expected of them. The professional has a responsibility to new recruits, to set high standards, and to lead by example. A professional has a duty to other professionals: eg to share new ideas or examples of good practice.

It is the duty of the IS/IT professional to provide leadership and guidance to the end-user community; a senior 'champion' for ethical issues is one idea worthy of further consideration.

The concept of an ethics advisor and/or advisory

The concept of an ethics advisor and/or advisory committee needs investigation. There is a real possibility that organisations can be persuaded that it is more profitable to correct a poor system than to release it onto the market. At the same time, though, there is a risk 'professionals' will stop thinking seriously about ethics, taking the view that it is the work of the advisors. Few would deny that professionalism is part of the answer to the ethical worries raised by ICT. However, the professionals are likely to be white, literate, middle aged or young, urban, not disabled, and men. The information age affects, and can be affected by very many more people than the professionals in the ICT sector.

The driving forces behind virtual education (VEd) were meeting with a number of practical constraints. The vision of VEd includes a 'global' education community introducing a variety of cultural approaches and attitudes to education. Issues such as mode of address, voice tone, attitude to assessment, language and understanding, and the type of pedagogical approach may have an impact on learning. The issues under discussion were wide ranging, but can be categorised under the headings of infrastructure, human factors in teaching and learning, and wider social implications. The infrastructure supporting virtual education is a combination of technological and human resources. The most pressing concerns are: technological capability; reliability; predictability; controllability; cost of access. It must be remembered that there is usually a considerable performance difference between institution-based resources and home-based resources.

There is a great deal of concern about the loss of face-to-face interaction. Education is characterised as "more than information or knowledge transfer". Even in established distance learning initiatives contact time is considered a vital ingredient. Face-to-face communication carries a wealth of subtle aids to mutual understanding, giving vital feedback to both tutors and students. Contact time between tutors and students is important to clarify misunderstandings, provide alternative explanations, correct incorrect assumptions, and to encourage and provide support to the student. Although text messages and/or video conferencing can be used in this way, these methods are not as efficient as face-to-face interaction: more time and effort may be needed on the part of both the student and the tutor to get the same results.

Face-to-face communication both between tutor and student, and students and their peers, is an important factor in the integration of students in a social world. Aside from the commonly voiced concerns with regard to isolation through extensive engagement with computers, learning is enhanced through informal and ad hoc discussion with others.

A predominant concern regarding technology-based learning is the question of equal access. It is obvious that economic factors and levels of literacy are constraints to equal access. Less obvious, in the UK at least, are cultural constraints and language barriers. Methods of teaching and approaches to learning vary between cultures. Learning can be inhibited in a cultural context that differs from that of the provider of the learning module. Most of the development of virtual education has been carried out from a western perspective, and uses the English language. Yet much VEd development aims to sell western education, through the English language, to other parts of the world. Combination of these factors are likely to widen the education gap, in contrast to the utopian picture of 'education for all' painted by the advocates of VEd.

The implementation of virtual education is still at an experimental stage. The three case studies summarised below consider different perspectives: operational; access; and questions of viability. There are a wide range of social and ethical implications inherent in the adoption of virtual education. The apparent emphasis on the problems and potential adverse consequences of education delivered via ICT is a reaction to the heady utopianism of advocates and initiators of virtual education. It arises from a desire to seek a balanced perspective. This is not to say that these concerns are in any way trivial—far from it. What is evident is that the vision of virtual education as the answer to education for all does not match the current reality, either in technical or human terms. A number of questions need to be answered, and myths exposed, before virtual education is taken up as the route to the promised land of education and lifelong learning.

Privacy Issues

A huge proportion of the information that drives the information age is derived from data that is about individuals, or can be linked to individuals. On top of this, it is easier than ever to store, duplicate, manipulate and communicate that data, which can take the form of text, images, and recordings of sound, video and at times even touch. It is also easier than ever to associate these data types with each other. It is technically easier than ever to quickly gather, and search, vast amounts of data about individuals.

The technologies that facilitate 'data mining' and matching large data sets are becoming ever more commonplace, with legally sanctioned crime and disorder partnerships and attempts to detect fraud resulting in new data matching programmes. One result of the increases in data collection and data mining is the practical possibility of data surveillance. This means that a human being can now be tracked across the globe by the data shadow they leave behind them.

As with so many other issues in life, the impacts of loss of privacy will not fall equally or equitably. Due to distinctive names, or less common skin colouring, or disability, some people are easier to identify than others - equally some people are easier to mistake for each other. Beyond simple identification, some people have more need for privacy than others. Not everybody is equally likely to be targeted as a potential victim by criminals. Similarly, well educated, articulate, native speakers of English are more able to pursue the legal remedies available to protect their privacy. Thus a key question is how to prevent abuse of data in the first place. The most worrying kinds of abuse seem to fall into two main categories:

— individuals seeking illegitimate personal gain, perhaps through criminal acts

— authoritarian governments seeking to control populations.

While there is legislation to protect privacy in very many jurisdictions, there is a mismatch between the size of these jurisdictions and the largely global nature of trade, especially in data for which the transport costs are so near zero. Thus global trade is threatened by data protection and privacy legislation formulated by one trading block if due regard is not paid to other trading blocks. Given the all-conquering power of global trade, it seems apposite to ask what degree of protection is feasible or acceptable in a technological age that demands greater data collection, provides for easier surveillance and provides increasingly limited scope for withholding information? Even if legislation remains of some practical use, it depends for its force in deterring breaches. Short of repressive enforcement, this will need those with access to data and influence over security measures to act responsibly.

Future technologies raise new issues about privacy. For example intelligent agents could be making decisions about highly sensitive personal data outside the human context that might be automatically implicit to any other human. Similarly, geographical information systems can have privacy implications when tied to systems monitoring physical mobility. There is a strong argument for an impact assessment whenever a new technology is developed that takes account of privacy effects, although it is not widely thought that it should be an absolute requirement in every case— research is needed on what form such assessments should take. Data protection laws, human rights and freedom of information legislation may have an impact, putting pressure on public bodies to release information about which there are privacy concerns.

2

Information Revolution and Digital Divide

Today, Information and Communication Technology (ICTs) disparities usually exacerbate existing disparities based on location such as urban-rural, gender, ethnicity, physical disability, age, and, especially, income level, and between "rich" and "poor" countries. The digital divide is not an isolated entity, but a complicated patchwork of varying levels of ICT access, basic ICT usage, and ICT applications among countries and peoples. The private sector has slowly spread technology to middle income groups, but on the whole they fail to see the developing world and underserved populations as viable markets that require targeted products.

Governments often tend to the short-term demands of their constituencies, but do not provide a coherent, long-term plan for prosperity and effective ICT integration, and a legal and regulatory framework that foster ICT use. Dealing with the digital divide is beyond the scope of any single initiative and technology is not a silver bullet for the world's problems. It is important for organizations doing community ICT projects to bring a global perspective and an entrepreneurial approach, and they must cooperate with like-minded efforts to tackle the range of problems collaboratively. There are some of the key elements necessary for integrating technology into society in an effective, sustainable way so that people can put technology to use to improve their lives.

ICT disparities are usually exacerbate existing disparities based on location, gender, ethnicity, physical disability, age, and, especially, income level, and between "rich" and "poor" countries. Measures of the digital divide exists in number and cost of PCs, phones, Internet hosts, Web sites, Internet users, residential/organizational/international Internet bandwidth, technical capacity, and advanced applications like e-commerce. The spread of Internet users among the world's population is much more unequal than that of the use of other ICT such as TV or telephones. The inequality of Internet usage is even bigger than the spread of GDP between the world's rich and poor countries. The monthly connection cost for the Internet in much of Africa exceeds the monthly income of a significant portion of the population. In nearly all developing countries, phone calls are charged by the minute, and are often extremely expensive.

Additionally, Web pages are becoming increasing graphic-heavy and "large" in terms of file size. The dominance of English, and especially U.S. content, makes it less useful to other countries. Additionally, non-English countries produce less local content making the Internet less relevant to their lives, and less of a tool of self-expression and local communication. Advanced uses of ICT such as e-commerce applications show even greater disparities than in basic access to computers.

E-commerce is dominated by the U.S. and to a lesser extent some European countries. The U.S. has 64% of all secure servers in the world; the next highest is the U.K, with only 5.32%, and the vast majority of countries have less than 0.1%. There is a wealth of real and anecdotal evidence of the digital divide. Wealthy nations comprise some 16 per cent of the world's population, but command 90 per cent of Internet host computers.

Of all the Internet users worldwide, 60 per cent reside in North America, where a mere five per cent of the world's population reside. One in two Americans is online, compared with only one in 250 Africans. In Bangladesh a computer costs the equivalent of eight years average pay. Ethnic and racial divisions in ICT use have been studied in the U.S., but are much less studied outside. Gaps also exist in adoption by gender, and the sector of disabled individuals show especially low levels of Internet use.

Major cities are far more likely to have Internet, phone, and PC access than smaller cities and rural areas. These gaps are even more significant given the fact that more than 50 percent--and as many as 80 percent--of the population in poorest countries, live in rural areas. The "number of users" online statistic is only a small part of the "digital divide". For practical reasons, current statistics focus on the raw numbers of PCs or numbers of people using a technology. They do not measure well how well people are using the technology, and whether the impact is positive or negative for themselves and their communities for business, educational, governance and social uses. While the current set of statistics can only provide rough estimates of how technology is used between countries and socio-economic groups, more than enough information is known to show that these divisions exist to spur reasoned action.

E-readiness assessment, combined with conventional "digital divide" statistics could provide this action plan. A deeper understanding of ICT use can be gained from the wealth of "e-readiness" assessments around the world. The e-readiness assessments seek to gauge how ready a country is to participate in the information economy or information society. In the process, the assessments draw upon many of the statistics used above as well as many more, including use of computers in schools and in healthcare.

National governments can play a fundamental role in creating an environment that will foster technology use and encourage national and international investment in ICT infrastructure, development, and a skilled workforce. These include telecommunications privatisation, standards setting, consumer protection, and government usage of ICT. Economic growth and social equity are both needed to bridge international and domestic digital divides. However, no consensus exists on exactly what policies are needed for either of these goals.

Many African and Middle Eastern countries seem to be far behind in policies needed to bridge international and domestic digital divides. There are a number of African countries with no registrar for their top-level country codes. The majority of countries with laws on electronic authentication have not yet developed detailed standards, although a number are working on them. At the same time, a number of projects geared for the developing world offer promising new technologies and adaptations.

India's "Simputer" and Brazil's "Volkscomputer" are often cited examples of locally produced, locally appropriate technologies that fit the needs and budgets of the developing world. Two developed world projects are also seeking to produce new "developing market" technologies—the MIT Media Lab, and HP's 1 Billion dollar E-Inclusion project. On the software side, India is the prime example of a country that has succeeded in developing a globally competitive IT sector—though the replicability of their success may be doubtful for other countries. Digital divide programmes are operated by organizations ranging from the smallest NGO to the largest multinational corporation.

Private telecentres provide telephone access for a fee. Some are adding fax, email, and Internet services, such as Senegal's micro-enterprise Phone Shops and Africa Online's "E-Touch" centres in Kenya. Donor-funded telecentres include such projects as the Nakaseke Multipurpose Community Telecentre in Uganda.

Digital Divide: Definitions

The gender divide will steadily decrease, at least in terms of users of the Internet. In South Africa for example, the number of women online recently surpassed the number of men. It can be reasonably expected that the ratio of women online in these countries will reach levels similar to the country's overall gender and power balances—which is often quite unequal, but should be considered in that larger context. Some small-scale ground-level projects show that computers can level the playing field for everyone and especially help people out of poverty. But on a country-wide level, and around the world, the statistics indicate that computers simply have not played that role.

Most countries could simply be shut out of the global competition, without the existing resources and investment to develop local ICT sectors; only a few countries may be able to develop strong ICT-fuelled economies. While the international and domestic digital divides may shift—including a few new countries and a slightly larger segment of society—the gulf between the "haves" and "have-nots" will deepen without adequate pro-active measures.

The term 'digital divide' may be taken at the broadest level to refer to the gap between those individuals and communities who own, access, and effectively use information and communication technologies (ICT) and those who do not. However, the term is often employed in a generalised way that masks its complex and diverse nature. This detracts from more informed and coherent debates surrounding its existence and extent. The definition has become unclear, and it is recognised that there are now multiple 'digital divides'. As the range of ICT and its capabilities increase, what constitutes a 'digital divide' and how to measure it become unclear. It is possible to dispute the size, characteristics and reality of its existence, and hard to clearly measure any progress made in reducing disparities. Clearer definitions and measurement criteria are needed in order assess the effectiveness of policies and initiatives. The absence of such criteria can leave policy initiatives open to criticism and difficult to defend. Divides can be seen to exist in relation to:

— ownership of new technologies

— access to those technologies.

However, issues of ownership and access are not as straightforward as they are often presented. For example, ownership does not necessarily equate with use, and ownership of household ICT does not necessarily mean that all individuals within that household own or use the technology. Thus, statistical accounts about the extent of the divide may be insufficient and may mask the complexities and extent of divisions. Similarly, ICT and internet access are largely devoid of qualitative understandings about the type and size of disparities.

— Type of technologies

— Age, capacity and functionality of devices

— The availability of technological and human support and resources to which different people have access.

However, as people obtain different levels and types of access in a number of different locations, divides can also occur on individual, educational, community and even wider demographic bases. There are definable gaps between:

— those who own state-of-the-art computers and subscribe to an ISP

— those who have access to computers and the internet at work, libraries or other locations and know how to use them

— those who have minimal access to computing technologies and few reasons for use

— those who have no experience of computer and information technologies.

The speed with which new technologies develop, coupled with wider societal differences, mean that it remains highly unlikely that complete parity will be attained. A clear and agreed indication of the levels and type of access sought and why these would be effective in reducing the divide(s) would be beneficial. 'Digital divides' involve a complex web of interconnected social, economic and cultural factors that cannot be fully captured by a definition that focuses solely on access or ownership. Whilst access is a key factor to be addressed in bridging the 'digital divide', it is merely one aspect.

Universal access to computers and the Internet is considered necessary to avoid social divisions and offer opportunities for all by ensuring that future 'knowledge economies' include everyone. Failure to bridge the divide may result in powerful digital communication tools exacerbating and entrenching societal disparities. As ICT continues to proliferate, the development of 'digital divides' may require the whole concept of poverty itself to be re-examined. Digital divides have repercussions in the following areas:

1. *Education and standards*: The proliferation of ICT in education and the expansion of Internet-based information and services further amplify the chasm between the information 'haves' and 'have nots'. Those on the wrong side of the divide(s) may have less opportunity to participate and engage with both formal and informal education, training and information. Changes in education are likely to mean that ICT skills will become the 'indispensable grammar of modern life' and a 'tool for lifelong learning'. Social inclusion and economic development in the 'Information Age' are mutually reinforcing, and for people in low income neighbourhoods, gaining and exploiting ICT skills lead to opportunities to participate fully in local and national economies.

2. *Economic competitiveness and employment*: Ninety per cent of new jobs in the UK require some degree of computing ability. In the US, it is estimated that around 60% of new jobs require 'advanced' technological skills. It is feared that demand for ICT skills will not be met by the adult population if ability levels do not increase significantly, particularly as the UK is currently the biggest e-commerce market in Europe. Failure to tackle the 'digital divide' and increase ICT skills could reduce the nation's ability to compete effectively in an increasingly technological global economy. Employers are increasingly considering ICT skills when recruiting staff and locating new businesses. American research also shows that those currently using ICT in their occupations earn significantly more and have better health levels.

3. *Social inclusion*: ICT skills and the ability to access technology facilitate a range of benefits that can be gained as electronically based products and services become accessible on line. Equality of access, skills and aspirations are essential to ensure that the gap between information rich and poor does not extend to gaps in access to electronically based participatory mechanisms. The digital divide constitutes the most pressing civil rights issue of the millennium. Exclusion can be reduced by using ICT to build and extend communication links and enabling improved access to information sources and services. However, failure to tackle divides in the immediate future may entrench inequalities further with ICT being most effectively used by the most advantaged groups.

Disparities in terms of the following must also be considered:

— *Content*: Does computer-based content that has equal relevance and value for all groups in society exist, or does content tend to reflect wider inequalities and power differentials. A number of more recent reports have highlighted how content can be a barrier to ICT engagement for many disadvantaged individuals and groups.. For example, The Children's Partnership suggest that one in five Americans faces at least one of the following content-related barriers.

  — *lack of local information* - material that is relevant and useful for specific under-served communities

  — *language barriers* - for instance, it is estimated on the basis of this research that 87% of all documents on the Internet are in English, yet a great number of individuals do not have English as their primary language, thereby leaving them in an inferior position in relation to advantages gained through uses of the Internet

  — *lack of cultural diversity* - there is a dearth of internet content created by ethnic minorities or organised around specific cultural interests or practices

  — *literacy barriers* - the vast majority of information on the Internet is written for an audience with average or above literacy levels, yet it is argued that over one-fifth of Americans do not have the necessary reading and writing skills to function effectively in everyday life

— *Literacy:* Certain levels may need to be achieved to use and benefit from a range of new technologies. Yet literacy levels are often left out of debates surrounding the 'digital divide'. Moreover, it is argued that new technological tools may require a consideration of a range of literacies that enable individuals to utilise them effectively. For example, the Bertelmann Foundation argue that aspects such as contextual literacy, media creativity, social competence and responsibility should be included. To incorporate these aspects presents formidable challenges in three key areas, namely education, workplace skills and civic engagement. Similarly, Carvin suggests that in terms of digital equity we should also consider issues beyond 'basic literacy' to include: functional literacy; occupational literacy; technological literacy; information literacy; adaptive literacy.

— *Pedagogy:* From an educational and occupational perspective, ICT may be of little use without effective training, curriculum and teaching. With much informal learning with and about ICT being undertaken in the home, the human and educational resources that individuals can draw upon in the home and cultural background become significant in discussions about the 'digital divide'.

— *Community:* Does the technology enable the development and spread of effective and strong communities on and off line? Are there disparities in the relevance, desires and needs for different communities to use ICT?

Whilst there is significant evidence showing the existence of a 'digital divide', there is no consensus as to whether it is remaining constant, is a narrowing and transient phase, or is indeed growing. Research shows the number of people owning and accessing ICT has increased significantly over recent years. This is illustrated by the growth in the number of internet users.

In UK, according to a 2001 ICT survey, thirty per cent of all households can access the Internet via a home computer, more than double the number identified in 1999. The number of over-55-year-olds and socio-economic groups C2DE on line is increasing rapidly. There has also been a decrease in the relative wealth of the 'average' user in recent years. One in 14 Internet users have already used mobile phones or digital TV to access the Internet. Access via digital TV is becoming an increasing possibility for a growing number of people as uptake has risen to around a quarter of all homes. Twenty-eight per cent of the respondents in one study felt that delivery through their TV would make them use the Internet more. Some evidence suggests that divides will decrease in the future. Children's use of home computers is increasing, as is the number of households where the child is the main PC user. Two-parent households with one or more children are most likely to have internet access.

Despite the increasing numbers owning and accessing ICT, there are still significant gaps between the 'information rich and poor', and closer analysis of evidence casts doubts over claims that 'digital divides' are narrowing. In UK, over half of the individuals in social grades AB are connected to the Internet at home. This is true for little more than 1 in 10 over-55s or social grades DE. Existing home internet users are more likely to have access in other locations, to have more informal information sources, and also to have access and use of other ICT in the country. There are groups of young people who are uninterested in ICT, and these are often from backgrounds where inequalities already exist.

Dimensions of Digital Divide

Digital divide has been identified along a number of dimensions. For some individuals and groups these may be interconnected and present multiple barriers to the effective use of ICT. Let us consider the situatiuon in UK.

1. *Socio-economic status*: In UK, in socio-economic profile DE the number of those who do not own or have never used a PC is double that of those in profile AB. Home internet access ranges from 53% amongst social grades AB down to as little as 12% in groups DE. Subscription rates for digital TV are also greater in the highest income group (31%) than they are for those in the lowest (14%). There are differences in the type and quality of hardware and software in households that may exacerbate inequalities further. There are qualitative divides in ICT use, with children from higher income backgrounds using home computers for a much wider range of activities than those from lower income families. Technology impinges upon the lives of the less privileged in a number of ways, yet is less likely to be fully understood or as effectively used.

2. *Employment status*: Over twice as many employed people are 'on line' than there are unemployed. Seventy-one per cent of employed compared to 32% of those not working were found to have a computer at home. Sixty-one per cent in social groups ABC1 compared to 28% in C2DE thought ICT was essential to their work. Those in rented property are less likely to have internet access than owner-occupiers. Four per cent of council tenants, compared to 22% of residents in high income areas, were found to have internet access. Other groups with lower-than-

average take-up are described as 'independent elders', 'blue collar owners' and 'Victorian low status'. Households with two adults and one or more children have internet access rates of up to 35%, whilst single-parent families access rates range from 7% to 11%.

3. *Gender*: Women are 14% less likely to have ever used a computer. They are 10% less likely to use one at home and 6% less likely to use one for work. Fifty-two per cent of men, compared to only 39% women, have access to the Internet, and 7% more men than women state they have access in the home. Boys own and use ICT more in the home than girls, and have more positive perceptions of their own ICT use and ability. Research identified that educational computing is constructed as a 'male' activity during classroom interactions. This can diminish participation and enthusiasm amongst girls and affect educational and occupational choices. Women and girls are also often under-represented, or represented stereotypically, in ICT media and content. Female use of ICT is related to wider societal structural inequalities and barriers to power, and discrimination against women in traditional pathways such as education and employment can lead to resistance to learning with ICT.

4. *Geographical location*: London (34%) and the South East (30%) have the highest regional rates of internet access. The North East (22%), Wales (20%), Scotland (19%) and Northern Ireland (16%) have the lowest. The majority of ICT-related economic and job opportunities are concentrated in London, the South East and in the regional capitals. Charges for

telephone calls may contribute to the structuring of ICT use based upon geographical location. Fewer incentives exist for companies to offer competitive services to rural areas. Fewer community-based projects, initiatives or training opportunities are offered in rural locations, due to the lower numbers of immediate residents. Distance and travel create further barriers.

4. *Ethnicity*: Many deprived neighbourhoods have high proportions of ethnic minorities, who have less access and ownership of ICT due partly to economic factors. Barriers exist to those whose first language is not English, as the majority of training, content and operating systems are in English. Certain literacy levels are necessary to benefit from ICT. Factors relating to culture impact upon use. Large variations in attitudes, use and experiences with ICT could exist between groups from various cultural backgrounds, but there is little research in this area.

5. *Disability*: Both computer use and internet access were found to be markedly lower amongst disabled people. Designers often fail to recognise the rights and access requirements necessary for people with disabilities. There is a wide range of disabling conditions that require specific approaches to ICT design and provision. Nonetheless, some core issues and barriers relevant to a number of cases include the following:

   — Hardware and software is generally not specialised or adaptable.

   — Lack of awareness: negative and incorrect assumptions are made about the levels of disabled people's achievements.

- There is a lack of resources, both real and perceived.
- Efforts for inclusion are diluted through segmentation of services and incoherent initiatives.

6. *Age*: The over-65s represent almost 20% of the population but are the group least likely to be connected to the Internet, or to subscribe to digital television. Internet use drops from 14% amongst the 64-75 age group to 4% for those 75 or over. Retired households are least likely to have internet access, with only an estimated 1% of those living alone ever going on line. Those over 55 are significantly less likely to own or use a PC and have fewer current or desired computer skills. A large proportion of older 'non acceptors' report having no interest in using a computer.

Causes of Digital Divide

The major factors which are contributing to the digital divide are:

1. *Shortcomings of the markets*: There is an argument that commercial providers target the most profitable segments of society first and unconnected sections last. There are no guarantees that market provision will deliver affordable ICT for all groups in society. Market-led provision may reach 'natural' saturation levels and inequalities may be exacerbated following new technical waves and inventions.
2. *Cost*: The cost of purchasing equipment, telephone costs, tuition and perceptions of costs have also been reported as barriers for non-internet users. Cheaper

calls (26%), unmetered free access (17%), and cheaper subscriptions would encourage greater internet usage amongst existing home users. The cost of internet use by children is a central concern for many families, particularly low-income groups.

3. *Lack of relevance, interest and aspirations*: A significant number believe ICT is not relevant to their lives. Fifteen per cent of all people have no interest in using the Internet. Over half of those unconnected state they will never get on line. The perceived lack of relevance has a socio-economic dimension. Many people still largely associate ICTs with the 'economic domain'. Individuals in higher socio-economic occupational categories are more likely to use ICT at work.The number of outlets for use in the wider community, or in employment locally, are factors that impact upon the perceived relevance of ICT. Children also develop their use of ICT in relation to its perceived relevance to their current social position, gender role and peer group culture. Poverty of aspiration and opportunity are factors that lead to the development of self exclusion and further inequalities. Perceptions of the utility of computers is mediated by individual family discourses, wider learning communities, and particular software environments. Use tends to supplement rather than transcend existing social arrangements.

4. *Lack of access and support*: Forty-two per cent of all 'non regular users' stated that the biggest obstacle to internet usage was lack of access to suitable equipment. Twenty-one per cent of all non-users lack the confidence and skills necessary to use the Internet. Fifteen per cent felt there was a lack of people to help them learn about ICT both in formal

and informal settings. This may be particularly true in deprived neighbourhoods.

5. *Lack of literacy*: Many people do not have sufficient literacy levels to use ICT effectively. This poses a particular problem for groups whose first language is not English. Most keyboards are in English and do not include characters used in some other languages. Common computer programs tend to use English-only instruction, and the information on the Internet is in predominantly English. Higher levels of illiteracy in deprived areas may severely restrict the numbers using public access points. Lack of computer literacy can compound this problem and also present a barrier to effective mobilisation in other contexts.

6. *Lack of joined-up approaches*: The 'digital divide represents one aspect of wider inequalities. The 'joined up' nature of social problems is one of the key factors underlying the concept of social exclusion. There is often little collaboration or communication between local projects, or strategic thinking across organisations and few mechanisms for sharing good practice.Community groups still struggle to find funding from 'one time-limited initiative to another'. The private sector is still largely absent from debates surrounding ICT and social inclusion in deprived neighbourhoods.

7. *Barriers to community access*: Learning in mixed groups at community access points can make some groups feel uncomfortable. Barriers may exist relating to location, opening times, lack of adequate child care, security, facilities for the disabled, ethnic minorities and the elderly. Unsustainable,

inconsistent, unsuitable and partial funding are barriers to community-based initiatives. ICT access points may be poorly promoted or marketed, and their role and content may lack a local focus. Access based around community technology centres is not sufficient, and efforts should be focused toward access based in the home.

Policies to Bridging Digital Divide

In national as well as internation levels, a number of initiatives and policies aimed at bridging the 'digital divide' are in operation, but as yet few independent evaluations are available. In UK, as an overall concept, the *UK online* initiative encompasses a number of themed strands of activity, including providing access and learning at newly established centres, offering low-cost computers 'within reach', putting all public libraries and schools on line and supporting businesses. *The Computers Within Reach Scheme* is currently running a pilot phase covering up to 35,000 individuals from deprived areas and claiming benefits, and providing them with recycled computers and associated peripherals. Up to 100,000 recycled computers will eventually be issued. *The Wired Up Communities Project* aims to put many homes in disadvantaged areas on line and assess how individual access to the Internet can transform opportunities by enabling access to work, training and leisure services. School children in 'Wired Up Communities' will be involved in schemes that push computer ratios significantly higher than the National Grid for Learning targets. UK's *National e-Learning Foundation* has been established with the clear aim of providing affordable, individual access to laptops for children, particularly those in deprived areas. Local foundations are being established to deliver laptop learning locally. Typically, these will be innovative partnerships between local charities, businesses and parents. Digital divides have no single, identifiable cause or effect. Many government initiatives, therefore, are integrated alongside broader concepts and policies that aspire to tackle deprivation and exclusion. *The Social Exclusion Unit* has been tasked to identify and report on the problems facing those in the most deprived areas and tackle social exclusion in the poorest neighbourhoods, and findings are incorporated into the *National Strategy for Neighbourhood Renewal*. Improving IT in these areas is identified as one 'key' area.

A sample of recommendations and suggestions that propose methods for tackling the 'digital divide' drawn from a range of sources and are loosely matched to the factors contributing to the 'digital divide' identified above are presented below.

1. *Supplementing/enhancing provision from the markets*:

— Raise awareness about the extent and dimensions of the divide to industry. This would help them to identify specific areas of product development and marketing as sales level out due to saturation.

— Give recommendations to software producers to develop products with more non-textual representation in minority languages, and for teaching English as a second language. Create partnerships to identify areas for product development and incentives for companies to design products specifically for excluded groups.

— Create further competition to provide cheaper services amongst telecommunications, software and resource companies.

- Promote the concept of corporate social responsibility within the IT industry to raise awareness and involvement.
- Further develop the market for resale and refurbishment of used IT hardware.

2. *Reducing costs*

- Further develop hardware lending and low-cost purchase schemes, particularly in disadvantaged communities and also for the benefit of other under-represented groups.
- Co-ordinate, develop and identify a range of low-cost technical solutions to access provision for all types of ICT. This would help to reduce the numbers who perceive ICT as unaffordable.
- Continue to develop a national infrastructure of low-cost or free access points in under-served communities, with future developments being informed by research findings pertaining to existing centres.

3. *Increasing relevance, interest and aspirations*

- There needs to be continued and active promotion that the 'digital divide' has to be overcome because it undermines the basic rights of every individual.
- Internet service and content providers to develop alternative perspectives to attract non-users and give clearer messages about how they can benefit from on-line activities.
- Develop a range of incentives to use the Internet, both financial and non-financial, and produce content and programmes that are of relevance to people's life and encourage skills acquisition.

— The provision offered should reflect the interests and make-up of the community it aims to serve. Attention and initiatives should focus upon helping and encouraging people to package the information they already have, present their own thoughts and knowledge, and find relevant outputs and uses.

— Opportunities to learn skills with people in similar situations and from similar backgrounds should be offered and promoted.

— Develop 'taster' courses that link ICT directly to other aspects of life relevant the communities involved.

— 'E-missionaries' such as teachers and students should be encouraged, or recruited, to train the 'unconnected'.

4. *Increasing access and support*

— Encourage businesses to pass on their technical and general commercial expertise to community groups during the development of initiatives, including the negotiation of better deals on hardware and software, help with marketing plans, and hands-on help and support.

— Home outreach, childcare provision and women-only groups should be provided to encourage greater numbers of women to participate, especially where cultural backgrounds restrain women's activities.

— The provision, extension and development of home-loan laptops should be considered and supported by other forms of support service.

— Develop the use of existing community resources and locations, including schools, in order to help offer further free or inexpensive access and training.

— Arrange 'drop in', and open access facilities geared to those with little or no prior ICT experience.

5. *Increasing literacy*

— Encourage and develop special language facilities in areas where there are relatively high instances of individuals whose first language is not English. Offer appropriate software and courses for those with limited literacy, and develop initiatives that combine support for beginners in the use of ICT alongside relevant language and literacy support, such as translation and interpretation.

— Meeting the information needs of non-English speakers should be promoted and content should be readily available in languages other than English. Developments in ICT and language fonts mean that it is reasonably inexpensive and easy to set up and provide information in many other languages.

6. *Increasing joined-up approaches*

— Councils and local authorities should have a duty to develop plans illustrating how the resources available in the local communities can be maximised through a joined-up approach. This would also require more comprehensive data gathering and collaboration with local community groups, which, if handled sensitively, could increase understanding about the needs of community groups and help to deliver provide communication and collaboration.

— Continue to tackle the 'digital divide' in tandem with wider aspects of inequality.

— Involve the private sector in community initiatives to build the social capital necessary for community groups to effectively mobilise ICT.

7. *Overcoming barriers to community-based access and use*

— Audit disadvantaged communities to establish their needs and requirements in terms of content, and promote initiatives that involve them in directly creating materials.

— Develop better policy and delivery design by identifying clear lines of responsibility for co-ordinating advice and help through a single communication channel to all those who wish to develop community focussed initiatives. A more 'joined up' approach would reduce the fragmentation that can create barriers to community participation.

— Allow plans and projects to evolve organically from the people they aim to help, but provide support mechanisms to scaffold the development of sustainable community projects.

— Identify and work with recognised information leaders within the communities. Undertake social mapping to find key individuals, community needs and interests.

— Attempt to lure existing ICT-related businesses into deprived communities, and support new community-based ones through a range of subsidies and tax incentives.

Asia-Pacific Meeting on Bridging the Digital Divide

The leading Inter-governmental regional telecommunications organisation, Asia-Pacific Telecommunity (APT), organised the Asia-Pacific Meeting on Bridging the Digital Divide & Preparation for WTDC-02 in New Delhi, India from 13 -16 February 2002. The meeting discussed the initiatives of APT member countries and other regional players from the Information and Communication Technology (ICT) sectors in bridging the digital divide and exchange of information in promoting partnerships, mobilization and sharing of resources.

ICT play an important role in achieving maximum synergy of efforts and added useful value to the users. These efforts in addition to other efforts at national, intra regional and inter regional levels will help in bridging the digital divide. The rapid improvement in technology such as Mobile SMS needs to be leveraged for bridging the digital divide in the rural and remote areas.

In this meeting, OECD presented a comprehensive paper of OECD Approaches to Policy for e-Commerce, ICTs and the Digital Divide. They outlined their work on electronic commerce, the DOT Force Action Plan, ICT for Development and OECD's The Way Ahead for cooperation. While emphasizing their work on the Digital Divide, they also presented some activities that engaged with measurement and indicators in promoting the Understanding of the Digital Divide. The presentation was concluded by stressing some ways ahead of OECD cooperation and by actively joining through its workshops and conferences initiatives like OECD Global Forum on the Knowledge-Based Economy, Asia, early 2003, OECD Centre for Co-operation with Non-Members,

Global Forum on the KBE, Emerging Asian Economy Programme, Latin America and China Programmes, Participation of OECD in work of other bodies and co-operation with other International Organisations and Contribution of OECD to international initiatives.

The advent of digital technology and Internet is overcoming the limits of space and time and at a lower cost. The extent of digital divide, in terms of lower Tele-density, as compared to other parts of the world while it accounts for almost 2/3rd of world population and highlighted the asymmetric distribution of Internet hosts, Internet bandwidth and TV distribution in the world. The need for building on the regional Internet bandwidth to route the traffic economically.

The big gap between the developed and developing countries and also within the region and expressed the need for an immediate action for development of ICT. A creative policy by having commitment, leveraging on the advantages to develop other sectors, prepare a national plan, have partnership between public and private sector, encourage infrastructure expansion and maintain focus of policy on market principle. The policy should focus on rural communication development taking into account scale of community, operability of facilities and the economic viability.

One participant in the meeting illustrated the status of women participation in the ICT sector and highlighted the existence of a gender divide. Only a small portion of the female population of Asian developing is digitally empowered and pointed out that women concentrated at lower skilled employment levels. While concluding he made the following recommendations that have been derived from an ESCAP group meeting:

— Access: Need to build Cybercafes, alternative sources of software that are cost competitive and there is also the need to have specific allocation in national budget;

— Encourage education and training using ICT;

— Creation of enabling environment by participation of gender equality advocates, resource allocation and gender accountability, monitoring and reporting requirement.

A participant from South East Asian Ministers of Education Organisation (SEAMEO) informed the participants about the activities of SEAMEO. He mentioned that 15 regional centres in various countries of Asia promoting education, health and other cultural activities. He illustrated the extent of divide that exists in the South East Asia region and mentioned the factors like economic development, available of infrastructure, availability of education and income level. Following are the SEAMEO recommendations:

a) SEAMEO infrastructure should be linked to Public Infrastructure;

b) Linkages with existing International and regional organisations should be established

c) Content and infrastructure should be increased simultaneously;

d) More focus should be given to improve the skill and Knowledge.

In the future, there will be a need to encourage ICT and informed that a task force has been setup to facilitate the development of SEAMEO program. The future course of action is to improve the Infrastructure, promote Cyber education and establish virtual library so that SEAMEO can act as an information hub. The challenges to the digital divide include the lack of national policies and strategies, lack of awareness and upscaling of the successful projects to national ones, use of different access models and non availability of low cost devices. The challenges relating to ethical use of ICT, standards setting, training needs and modules.

Developing countries can use ICT to bridge the social divide in much better way. Working with partners to access global trust fund for supporting ICT infrastructure, building human capacity and extending use. Market failure in this area is still pervasive and there is, therefore a need for public involvement. There is lack of legal and institutional framework. There is need to stimulate local entrepreneurship and set the national policies. She also highlighted the problems of brain drain. UNDP is proactively working on analysing the potential of ICT to address social inequities.

The main policy areas of ILO, which included ensuring information economy becoming a job economy, need for ICT to become tool for development and key challenges facing education and training. On the whole there was greater gains with the introduction of ICT. ILO mentioned that investment, improving aceessibility, quality, training, fostering enetrprise and entrepenuership are necessary. In the Indian context, ILO is trying to push the report forward through a tripartite effort and trying to analyse the impact of automation.

One participant explained that Grameen Telecom (GTC) program is making efforts to bridge the digital divide in Bangladesh through handheld simple IT devices. It provides micro credit for the purpose.

Grameen Telecom was established in 1995 and is now a success. He also introduced the Telecom Scenario in Bangladesh and explained the relationship of GrameenPhone and its relationship with Grameen Telecom.

The Village Phone Program started in 1997. At the beginning of February 2002, the number of Village Phones stood at 9754 covering 8,637 villages out of the 68,000 villages in Bangladesh. The monthly average earning amounts to US$ 100 per month, which has helped in changing the social and economic status of the Village Phone ladies and their villages. He explained the role that Grameen bank plays by acting as a first point of contact.

GTC's future plan to have 50,000 village phones connecting equal number of villages by 2004 and upgrading a number of those into Village E-Mail and Telecom Centres (VETC). These VETCs will act as the building blocks to extend other I-T enabled services such as Tele-Medicine, Tele-education, weather, business and market information.

Mr. S.R.Das, Department Of Information Technology, India, emphasised on the digital unity brought about by I-T between freedom and distance. He informed the observation of the Working group on I-T, which includes introducing new opportunities and briefed on the recommendations that include Infrastructure development, e-Governance, education, rural development, Indian languages for Internet & standardisation and improving mass awareness.

Some of the initiatives that have been taken by the government include promotion of Internet access, creation of content with multimedia techniques,

Telemedicine and health care, IT applications for disabilities, Mass IT campaigns, technology development of basic tools and preserving cultural heritage. The recent achievements have been the computerisation of land records, national program on Low Cost Multimedia Content Creation, computerisation of Braille system and Computer Aided Tools for Celebral Plasy affected people, initiation of Tele-Medicine Projects, opening of Community Information Centres in North Eastern India and adult literacy programs. Prof. Jhunjhunwala started his presentation by introducing briefly the status of Telecom in India. He emphasised on the need for making the services affordable.

Speaking about the affordability, he mentioned that only 3% of household could afford the present cost per line and emphasised that this percentage can be significantly increased by reducing the cost to around $200. He introduced the CorDECT technology developed by IIT, Chennai that supports voice and Internet at a price of $US 200 and covers around 25Kms in rural area. He informed that this technology is deployed in India and also in a number of countries.

Prof. Jhunjhunwala also introduced n-logue, which focussed on rural areas only. He highlighted the success story of STD PCOs which account for 25% revenue and around 800,000 entreprenuership and low cost Cable TV ($2 per month). He emphasized on the need for Local Service Provider and having public access. Introducing low cost kiosks, he mentioned that the total cost for the entreprenuer is only $1000. He also informed the participants about various pilot projects going on.

The SchoolNet Thailand project, which connects 4200 schools to the Internet. The project is a joint effort of

Ministry of Science, Communication Technology and Education and promotes awareness, promotion of content development, training of teachers, providing access and promotion of classroom activities. The access to Internet is free of Charge. For creating content the concept of digital library was introduced that covers seven academic subjects.

A digital library schoolkit was provided to teachers for developing library material. The contents developed for archieves were indexed and a suitable Search engine was also developed. The project evolved in the years 1995-97 and is currently under development stage. In the forthcoming years the project will be expanded to include more schools, more number of web sites and larger bandwidth.

Japan's initiative for bridging the digital divide mentioned that we are witnessing an era of ICT revolution. He introduced the current status of Internet user in Japan. The total number of users currently are 42 Million and the household penetration is about 37%. In Japan, the number of Mobiles (72 Million) has exceeded the number of fixed, which is about 61 Million. 68% of these mobile customers access the Internet. He informed the participants about the governments national plan of e-Japan to become world's most advanced ICT nation by 2005. The priority policy areas include Ultra high speed network infrastructure to 30 million households by 2005, e-Commerce Rules and Infrastructure, realisation of e-Governance by 2003 and Human resource Development.

There are many types of digital divide such as those based on geography and those based on age and physical disability. For the process of bridging the digital divide, Japan has identified five priority areas relating to formulation of most advanced infrastructure, education & HRD, e-Commerce, digitization of Administration and Security and Reliability uses. The Japan initiative also informed about government initiatives of fair competition & Pro-competitive policies and establishment of Broadband network. He also informed the participants about the support to operators in terms of finance, special loans, tax reliefs, construction of Base Station by local operator etc. to encourage roll out.

Ms. Suriah apprised the participants of the profile of Malaysia and the policy thrusts that included Infrastructure development, Infostructure development and Industry development. The direction of efforts is to achieve the 2020 vision that Malaysia beholds.

Malaysia has a Cyber law to facilitate e-Commerce and protection of consumers. The market has been open to competition and Universal Service supports are envisaged for funding some of the initiatives. In 2000 a new converged regime has been implemented. A set of targets has been developed for the year 2005 laying down the key indicators. Ms. Suriah described the Multimedia initiatives like Multimedia SuperCorridor and mentioned that plans are on to roll it out to other parts of the country.

A Universal service Provision (USP) policy has been approved by the government. The government's contribution for the 8th Plan is a total of US$ 250 Million for Universal Service as it considers that the targets would be difficult to achieve by market forces only. There are plans of infrastructure development to schools and provision of Telecentres. Besides the government contribution, there are also contributions from Service Providers. She informed the participants about MCMC, which is an effective regulator with the necessary flexible and autonomous authority. She identified the challenges of bridging the digital divide, building the critical mass and e-culturalisation.

Another partipant in Japan presented the various satellite based initiatives for communication and disaster management. Many disaster areas are still devoid of access to modern tools. He explained how this project will be able to manage, monitor and mitigate disasters through timely information communication from different mobile and airborne terminals.

Mr. Shafiee informed the participants of the initiatives taken by IRAN towards the TOKYO declaration plan. He emphasised on the need for larger private sector participation.

A national ICT plan was approved specifying specific targets of roll out of various services including Internet. The charges for Internet has been reduced. Pilot projects have been initiated to improve e-Commerce. Special efforts are being taken to promote distance learning, virtual library, e-Governance and education. Iran is co-operating with Regional development organisations to promote ICT. Mr. Ahmed started with a brief overview of demographic and technological scenario in Maldives. He informed about the plans to introduce competition in Maldives and enumerated the current subscriber trends.

Some of the challenges to the growth of ICT are closed markets, high prices, lack of high speed, small market and low teledensity. The policy initiatives to take up this challenge include opening up of ISP market, deployment of Multipurpose Telecentres, available of telephones at discounted rates for public access centres, holding of Internet fairs, Free Internet Account, reduction of import duty on computer and introduction of IT in educational Curriculum. Ms. Dugarmaa informed the participants about the level of Telecom development in Mongolia including the number of exchanges, telephone lines and PCOs.

The private participation in ISP was opened in 1994 and as on 2001 thre are 7 ISPs and 10000 subscribers. In the area of Mobile Services, 2 joint venture companies are operating. She also informed that a separate regulatory body has been established and a Universal Service Fund has been created. The Policy aims to provide a teledensity of 15 in Ulanbator and 10-12 in the provinces, provide reliable access and Internet access to 50% of population. Ms Dugarmaa also detailed various policy objectives and ICT projects going on in Mongolia.

A participant in Bangladesh, identified the impediments to the bridging the divide as Lack of Education, fear of technology use, economic conditions, lack of english education, pressure of family responsibility and prevalent social and cultural aspects. He mentioned about various problems pertaining to infrastructure. BTTB has plans to provide telephones in rural areas using VHF and Cellular Mobile, The long terms plans include a submarine optical linking nationwide OFC newtork, liberalising satcom policy in 2010, project to provide at least one telephone in a village and educating the youths. India enquired whether BTTB sees a co-operation in Bangladesh and West Bengal province in India.

The policy of the government to encourage local and foreign investors to compete and cooperate in the investment for construction, development and expansion of telecommunications network. He detailed the policy plans formulated for the development and various targets laid down in the development Plan.

Mr. Choudhary from IBM mentioned that digital information is fast changing the behavourial needs of the society. The digital divide has four drivers, viz., Technological, Social, political and economic drivers, the impact of which were illustrated by the speaker using statistical evidence. Mr. Choudhary discussed initiatives on how can the government compete in the global market place. He expressed the need for integrating the front-end to the legacy.

The focus has to be on customer centric applications and services. He called on the government to understand the business and take concrete steps thereon to move towards integration. Mr. Sawhney provided an example of health care using pervasive computing, which can be quite effectively used as a Tele-Medicine tool for real time integration.

In India, there are about 600,000 villages with 91% having population less than 2000. The rural areas lack in infrastructure, have agriculture based economy and call for heavy income without matching return. New Telecom Policy has now laid down specific targets of rural telecommunications that include teledensity targets, provision of village public telephones, provision of Internet to every district headquarters. The rapid development has taken place due to indigenous efforts and enquired whether the Cyber dhabas are managed by BSNL or individuals. The size of the digital divide in India adds new challenges.

A participant from Zurriyadi highlighted development of public access to government, HRD, development of content and application as the three elements of e-Government. He introduced the concept of Information System Solution for Autonomous Region which provides various e- Services from Community Access Centres and Community learning centres.

SIMTAP, a web based public system was introduced in Takalar in Indonesia, which has resulted in productivity increase. He also made a proposal to APT from Indonesia to contribute towards a pilot project for introducing e-Governance to improve quality of service, introduce e-learning and develop SMEs.

3

Access to ICTs and Electronic Economy

During the late 15th and 16th Century in Europe, the spread of knowledge triggered by Gutenberg's printing press both helped to drive, and was supported by, a continent-wide rivalry of religious ideas. Now, the Internet has become both the fuel and the vehicle for a dramatic spread in democracy, intensifying demand for and supporting the spread of genuinely transparent and participatory and more efficient systems of government at both the national and global levels.

The number of democracies worldwide has doubled in little more than a decade. But in too many countries, institutions remain fragile, services are weak, officials unaccountable. And the lack of a democratic dividend-in terms of jobs and better services-has been undermining public faith in these new systems, particularly among the poor. ICT offers real hope in all these areas, offering greater citizen input into decision-making and better social services for all. From the Philippines to Zimbabwe, we have seen over the past year how cell-phones and e-mail have been used to gather supporters and spread ideas and information across grassroots and global networks with dramatic effect.

ICT is also proving a vital tool in helping link new civil society networks around key issues, from global warming to women's empowerment to attempts to make globalization more responsive to the needs of developing countries and the poor. ICT can also make government services and institutions cheaper, more efficient and more accessible. Developing countries like Brazil and Chile already have successful experiments underway in these areas.

In parts of India, online government licensing is cutting through traditionally tortuous bureaucracies. There is little point talking about the impact of ICT on democracy and development in countries where ICT barely exists. Just 0.4 percent of Africans and South Asians have used the Internet, compared to over half of North Americans. So the first challenge in harnessing limited resources is to identify the strategic levers of change that best help countries to boost the spread and application of ICT.

Human Development Report 2001 argues, governments need to put in place an enabling environment that encourages investments in hard-ware and tertiary education. A Digital Opportunity Initiative study that UNDP recently undertook with Accenture and the Markle Foundation shows the need for developing countries to put in place comprehensive national e-strategies that address issues such as connectivity, regulatory environment, and human capacity.

Usually a well-educated technically-qualified pool of potential IT employees is a more critical advantage than the quality of a country's telecom infrastructure. This revolution really is about people. Helping countries to move forward in these ways will be a central feature of our Global Network Readiness initiative that we are rolling out first in Bolivia, Romania and Tanzania. Estonia is one of the world's best examples of how much can be achieved with the right enabling environment.

That country's Tiger Leap project, sup-ported by UNDP, wired the entire coun-try starting in the early 1990's and has ensured that the current generation of Estonian student is 100 percent computer literate. Tiger Leap has also been a catalyst for regional economic development and provides access points across the country, which citizens can use to conduct most of their transactions with the government. Almost all government documents-as well as Real Audio broadcasts of parliamentary sessions-are available online. Other countries should follow Estonia's lead. The global surge of democracy is real but fragile. And ICT can help consolidate the gains of the past several decades.

The new information and communication technologies (ICTs) are the outcome of technological development, and the digital divide is the inevitable consequence of income differences. Admittedly, today, the people of developed countries have a greater access to the benefits of technological progress as their incomes increase, but a number of techniques also represent tools for human development which enable the population to improve its income and its life expectancy, to enjoy better health and living standards, and to be more innovative.

Like education, technology represents a means for the poor to surmount their condition. It therefore represents a tool for growth and development and is not only an outcome of them. The United Nations

Millennium Declaration signatories' leitmotiv "[to undertake] among other things, to ensure that the advantages of the new technologies, and in particular ICT, should be granted to all", should be viewed in this context. Access to information, and to knowledge acquisition, is viewed as crucial for the development process. On one hand it involves the existence of adequate ICT networks and services, on the other hand, the capability to use these tools in order to design applications useful to the whole of society. However, both these tools and the capacity to use them are unequally distributed". The Millennium Declaration acknowledges the specific problems faced by the vulnerable communities such as least developing countries (LDCs), the small developing insular states and landlocked countries. It also acknowledges the necessity to enable these countries to fully participate in the world economy.

The vulnerable communities are, even to a larger extent than the others, dependent on ICTs because of their isolation. Indeed, in spite of considerable progress achieved in recent years, access to ICTs, namely to the fixed and mobile telephone, the Internet and to radio - broadcasting, remains unequally distributed. The double-speed development is particularly felt in Africa, the continent which contains 39 out of 49 least developed countries in the world. According to the International Telecommunications Union (ITU) 1991 estimates, total telephone penetration represented 49 per cent in the developed countries, against 3.3 per cent in the emerging countries, and only 0.3 per cent in the least developed countries.

The large-scale diffusion of the new ICTs in developing countries appears as an unavoidable challenge to be met. Should "the digital divide " which can currently be observed persist, developing countries could become even more isolated from economic circuits, and extremely marginalized, and their takeoff opportunity once more heavily at stake. This situation entails, once more, that the issue of the means to be implemented and the mechanisms to be promoted in order to help these countries to become less isolated and benefit from the progress in the new information technologies, and to integrate them in the global exchanges be addressed.

The necessity to bring in the relevant support so as to enable these countries to benefit from economic globalisation is largely recognised and established. According to this stance, the debate can take place at the level of the analysis of the fundamental constraints, the determination of the potential for the improvement of institutional and human capabilities, taking into account existing mechanisms, and finally the definition of an appropriate strategy based on specific national, regional and international needs.

The LDCs are defined as low income countries whose growth has been hampered for a long time, in particular by a low level of human resources development, and/or serious structural problems. These countries are included in a list established by the United Nations General Assembly, which is revised on a three-year basis. There are currently 49 LDCs in the world, of which 34 are to be found in Africa, with a population of 427 million, living, according to the United Nations, on less than one dollar a day. Most analysts consider that LDCs' situation has worsened, which has resulted in a limited growth of the telecommunication sector.

The problems are on one hand technical, linked to the telecommunications services obsolescence and under-equipment, on the other hand political, with geographical discrepancies resulting from political choices implemented in general by centralising States which promoted a more or less exclusive concentration of telecommunication services in the capital cities. However, the future information society assumes a universal and equal access to all the populations in a country. The main obstacles and bottlenecks should be looked for in the following fields: infrastructure status, the financial and institutional capabilities, and the level and qualification of human capital, cultural differences, etc.

The discrepancy between development levels in Africa, and more particularly in the least developed countries, and levels attained in the rest of the world has widened in the field of ICTs more than for more classical criteria used for measuring development. The fact is that African population in its large majority has never made a telephone call, or in terms of quality of communication, because of existing networks obsolescence or saturation. Irregular power supply, if any, a common feature to the whole of the landscape represents a major hindrance to an intensification in the use of ICTs, especially out of the large towns.

Many countries' power distribution networks are very limited and penetration in rural areas has just been initiated. Long power cuts are more or less the norm, even in such capital cities as Accra or Dar es Salam. Further, most tax regimes continue to consider ICT products, almost exclusively imported, as luxury goods, which makes their purchase price even more expensive, thus preventing most people from buying them. Under these conditions, it is not surprising that radio -

broadcasting still remains the most widely used mass communication means, and the ownership of a radio set is much more common than any other electronic device. It is also worth observing that many people listen to or watch the same TV set at the same time.

According to the 2001 UNESCO Report the existing radio transmission networks reach more than 60 per cent of the sub-Saharan African population, while television coverage is essentially limited to the larger towns. However, it can be said that most LDCs are experiencing an expansion and a modernisation of their telecommunication networks, which is reflected in an annual increase of the number of main lines of around 10 per cent. In addition, a large part of the telecommunication network is analogue and a large number of sectors operate to capacity saturation or they are not very reliable, especially during the rainy seasons.

Moreover, 50 per cent of the available lines are concentrated in the capital cities, where only 10 per cent of the population live. Compared to the rest of the world, it appears that the region avails of by far the least developed infrastructure. The existing telephone networks status varies greatly depending on the countries. Some, like Botswana and Rwanda, which have made telecommunications one of their priorities, are installing digital switches with optical fibre links between towns together with the most up to date cell and mobile telephone technology.

At the other extreme, countries such as Madagascar and Uganda have analogue telephone systems which, in general, are not very reliable and poor national links between urban centres. Thus, in terms of main lines capacity, the change which took place in the 90s shows considerable discrepancies from one country to another, since in some countries capacity decreased while in other countries it increased 300 per cent. The countries whose capacity stagnated are obviously those in which the political and economic situation have experienced serious problems in the past decade such as Liberia, Rwanda, Congo, Angola etc.

Conversely, neither are countries where the situation experienced the greater improvement characteristic of an average situation; in general, growth took place in small countries where networks development cost is much lower, such as in Cape Verde. At the sub-regional level, Sahel and Central African countries, such as Mali, Niger and the Democratic Republic of Congo, have less than two telephone lines per 100 inhabitants. With the advent of the mobile telephone, access to telecommunications increased considerably.

Uganda enshrines the example of the mobile telephone revolution in LDCs. This east African country granted in 1998 a licence to a second national operator (MTN Uganda), whose priority was access to prepaid mobile telephones. Microwave network installation is rapid and, in a country where the majority of the population cannot afford a subscription, prepayment makes telecommunications more easily affordable to many. The results were spectacular.

In slightly more than one year, MTN became the most important operator in the country. The company has since actively undertaken to expand the network to the rural areas. More than 50 per cent of the population and about 80 towns are currently covered by the cell phone. An increasing number of LDCs are now implementing the Uganda project.

The Internet is still a privilege in the least developed countries, where two out of a thousand inhabitants use it. This ratio, which is clearly less than the average of other developing countries is well below certain developed countries, where one out of four inhabitants has access to the Internet.

The Internet requires excellent quality and very fast connections, and the corresponding infrastructures. But, in the major part of these countries, especially landlocked territories and remote islands, there are very few national and international links.

These countries are not yet equipped with optical fibre links, and satellite links are limited and very expensive. Furthermore, internal telecommunication infrastructures are, generally speaking, concentrated in a few of the larger towns, while they are seriously insufficient in rural areas. As a remedy to this situation, certain countries have made the decision to supply access to the Internet via local call over the whole of their territory through the use of a determined zone code.

An additional characteristic of LDCs' situation is the difficulty in bearing the cost of the use of communication technologies. Indeed, the proportion of the population that can afford to pay the price of a telephone is much lower than in other countries.

Human poverty and institutional fragility deepen the gap between technologies adapted to the incomes and capabilities of rich and poor countries alike. Furthermore, revenue generated from international calls, especially incoming calls represents more than half the telecommunications revenue, while it also represents a source of foreign currency.

The main obstacles to the implementation of national information and communication services are listed below:

(1) lack of adequate standards for homologation of materials prototypes;

(2) difficulties in obtaining authorisations to have access to international telecommunication companies;

(3) lack of an appropriate legal framework for the creation of companies or value-added services suppliers' associations;

(4) lack of support services, computer training, information strategies planning;

(5) difficulties in obtaining the required funding;

(6) delay in the provisions relative to intellectual property rights;

(7) restrictions on freedom of speech;

(8) lack of satisfactory management and coordination mechanisms at the national, regional and subregional levels;

(9) lack of awareness of the importance of the implementation of the information and telecommunication infrastructure.

A study carried out UNCTAD, on electronic commerce development in ten LDCs, the most important obstacles mentioned by companies wishing to start electronic commerce in LDCs are of a regulatory character: foreign exchange control, telecommunications monopoly, restrictive commercial practices, miscellaneous prohibitions with respect to encryption, Internet telephony, and the possibility to use their own access portal, and so on.

While the use of a fixed telephone does not require any prior training, handling a mobile phone is already more complex; Furthermore, the poor level of technological knowledge in LDCs should also be taken into consideration. Certainly, the Internet provides access to the whole of global information, but one needs to be able to read and write in order to use a complex system and retrieve what one is looking for.

LDCs are not only the countries where per capita income is the lowest, but where the illiteracy rate is the highest, the enrolment rate in primary education is the lowest, and the educational divide between girls and boys the widest. Although an improvement of competence has been achieved in the last twenty years in certain deprived countries, some countries do not avail of the adequate capacities as yet. This shortcoming makes them incapable of adapting the technologies available in the world at large to their needs, and a fortiori to extend the use of ICTs and define their own programmes in order to meet their needs. Policies and instruments have been implemented in most countries in order to promote human resources development.

In the education and training sector varying levels were achieved in different countries. Indeed, in certain countries the efforts have resulted in human resources development in IT both in the formal academic system and in training institutions while in some other countries the performance levels remain poor. In addition, policy implementation faces difficulties, which are generally associated with hardware and software acquisition and shortage of a qualified workforce. The risk of cultural colonisation by nations producing most of the cultural goods on information highways is real, and exposes ICTs to being rejected by developing societies. The greatest handicap, which represents an inhibiting factor is the fact that, gradually, a certain "cyber-culture" is settling on the network with a specific behaviour, and with particular standards and languages.

Since the 1995 G7 Information Society Conference expressed its concern in respect of the digital divide dividing industrial countries from developing countries, and launched an appeal for "a shared vision of human empowerment", issues related to the digital divide have become an international priority. During the Okinawa Summit in July 2000, the G8 prepared the Okinawa Chart on the Global Information Society and created the Digital Opportunity Task Force (DOT Force).

The DOT Force designed a plan, "Digital Opportunities for all: Surmounting the Challenge ", presented during the G8 Summit in Genoa in July 2001. On the occasion of its Millennium Session, the United Nations General Assembly paid specific attention to ICTs, and a United Nations working group on ICTs was created, as a practical step, in order to reinforce the United Nations system role and leadership, and to develop effective partnership with the private sector, civil society and other relevant parties.

The ECOSOC session in July 2001 took up the theme of ICTs, with special emphasis on knowledge networks. The financing implemented by the international cooperation in ICTs clearly shows the importance given by the international community to this sector.

Among the United Nations agencies, the International Telecommunication Union (ITU), plays a key role in telecommunication development and the dissemination and exchange of information, in particular through its Telecommunication Development Bureau and the Strategy and Policy Unit. The World Bank, which offers assistance in the telecommunications field and ICT development. The United Nations Conference on Trade and Development (UNCTAD) has made Africa the priority region for the next two years. A financial commitment of 30 million Euros was obtained from the European Union for networks regional development for the improvement of local trade in Africa. UNESCO gives a high priority to initiatives in informatics and telematics in Africa through support to the Regional Informatics Network for Africa (RINAF).

In addition, UNESCO implemented the Creating Learning Networks for African Teachers project designed to help teacher training familiarise themselves with ICTs and their application in teaching, and to connect them to the Internet. The project, already operational in Zimbabwe, has been initiated in Senegal, and will be, in principle, extended to other African countries. In recent years, UNDP has launched several initiative and partnership agreements with the private sector and some foundations.

The UNDP Sustainable Development Programme for the Creation of Networks (SNDP) includes ten operational nodes in Africa (Angola, Benin, Cameroon, Malawi, Morocco, Mozambique, Chad, Togo, and Tunisia. National projects implemented within SNDP are funded for a two or three year period, and should, in principle, provide starting capital to launch a sustainable operation, either through remunerated services or incorporation to the State budget. The United Nations Programme for the Environment (UNPE) Mercury Project which utilises the VSAT (Very Small Aperture Terminal) technology for the implementation of an information exchange network on the environment in Africa.

Catalysing Access to ICT's in Africa (CATIA), initiated by the U.K. Department for International Development. CATIA has several objectives including support for key organizations influencing regulatory policy in the telecommunications and Internet sectors and CATIA will also encourage private/public partnership activities that facilitate low cost Internet access opportunities across Africa. In addition, UNESCO implemented the Creating Learning Networks for Africa Teachers project designed to help teacher training familiarize with ICTs and their application in teaching, and to connect them to the Internet.

Since 1973, ITU has significantly assisted LDCs. Currently, the 49 LDCs receive a technical assistance in various fields in order to accelerate the pace of development in their telecommunications, which, in turn, will entail socio -economic development in these countries. In conformity with the Buenos Aires Action Plan, and subsequently the Valetta Action Plan, crucial priorities include the introduction of new technologies, the reform and restructuring of the telecommunications sector, rural telecommunications development, human resources development, and telecommunications networks extension funding through partnership.

The main objective of these special actions towards LDCs is closing the digital gap between the poorest 49 countries and the rest of the world. In practical terms, the programme aims to increase average teledensity up to five main lines per 100 inhabitants, and connections to the Internet to 10 users per 100 inhabitants by 2010. The strategy will consist in focusing on a small number of countries, starting with those with the least means, and gradually covering the others.

A special assistance is equally brought to LDCs, which have just emerged from war, internal troubles or natural disasters, such as Somalia, Rwanda, Burundi, Liberia and East Timor. The aim of the assistance is to consolidate their political and regulatory frameworks in the telecommunication sector and to improve access to rural areas to services by encouraging private investment. The World Economic Forum (FEM) which launched, in April 2000, a global digital initiative to make the digital divide an opportunity for growth and which adopted an action plan in October 2001.

Within a development strategy, the ICT objective consists in allowing LDCs to benefit from these technologies in order to achieve the objectives of their collectivity/community in social, economic, educational and health care development. Some priority problems delay LDCs development including health and education; ICTs represent some of the possibilities for their resolution.

UN General Assembly states that it is urgent to utilize knowledge and technology potential in order to implement the objectives of the Millenium Declaration and find efficient and novel means to put this potential in the service of development for all. The main challenge is linked to the danger of creating a two-speed society in which only one part of the population has access to the new technologies, and is able to use them with ease, and enjoy the advantages they procure.

There is then a risk of a rejection of the new information culture and its tools. Hence, the preparation of LDCs for the advent of the information society is a priority task. Teaching, training and awareness building will necessarily play a central part. The opportunities offered by the global information and communication revolution to developing countries are considerable if adequate policies are correctly implemented. Indeed, the advantages of the new ICTs are no longer limited to the communication and information sectors; they now represent general use technologies, penetrating all fields and sectors, for instance :

a) *In the field of education*: ICT use has potential promise for drastic cost reduction and for an improvement of training and education quality. Education and training should be considered as a priority for the promotion of equal opportunity for participation in and benefit from the information Society. ICT integration in the curriculum and in teachers' education and training should be reinforced as teachers are knowledge multipliers in ICT use. Technological skills acquisition in all levels of education, especially the broadening of knowledge in informatics, is essential for attracting investment, and sustains entrepreneurship, which are both crucial for economic development.

b) *In the field of health care*, ICTs will play an important part in the alleviation of certain problems, which can be achieved by improving access to health care services in rural areas, by extending public education campaigns in order to promote sanitary behaviour, through the transfer of diagnoses information to the specialized centres, by reinforcing information for decision making, promoting information exchange between researchers and students, and valorizing public health establishments.

c) *In business*, where exchanges are hindered by poor transport and communication networks and lack of information, ICTs will allow business companies to become more competitive thanks to updated and adequate commercial information. Indeed, ICTs boost the establishment of links between chambers of commerce, commercial companies, and commercial associations and firms, so as to help small and medium-sized firms and develop regional and international exchanges, and further reduce the cost of business transactions.

d) *Food security*: for example, ICTs are a way of receiving drought alarms on time, enabling the timing of the planting of crops to be modified, thereby reducing the risk of famine.

e) *Women and development*: ICTs provide access to information and indicators which help in identifying problems. They provide equitable information opportunities for women, together with access to technology and technical education.

f) *Culture*: the new opportunities are numerous, including saving the cultural heritage on electronic media, supporting it with documents and carrying out its diffusion, and the original production of local contents.

g) *Development of governmental services*, as well as electronic registration of marital status and tax forms, for example.

The African countries' ICT needs listed in the New Partnership for Development in Africa (NEPAD) represent a significant reference point. The various studies carried out agree on the notion that the building an information and communication sector requires the utilisation and development of the following elements as supporting factors prior to the implementation of an ICT policy:

(1) a legal and institutional framework,

(2) human resources,

(3) technological infrastructures, and

(4) information resources.

LDC social and economic development is, to a large extent, determined by the size and quality of the employed population - its human and intellectual capital - education, training, and the valorisation of human resources will represent milestones for the new information society.

Furthermore, on one hand human resources development requires novel attitudes from decision-makers and new skills among both the executives and the labour force, i.e. the capacity to adapt, adopt and utilise the new technologies and master change, and, on the other hand, the creation of new labour markets in which the technical competence and knowledge acquired could be used.

No information and communication system can operate efficiently without reliable inexpensive and abundant technological means, in the form of computers, software and all the elements of a telecommunications infrastructure allowing data and information processing. Not only will it be necessary to modernise and develop the infrastructure and the telecommunications material and logical network at the national level, especially in rural and remote areas, but also to improve interconnection at the regional level and include international transit centres for access to international telecommunications networks.

The poor are solely beneficiaries of information and knowledge technology. It is obvious that this is not the case. Deprived communities produce their own information and knowledge. Thus, ICTs may play a positive part by allowing the wider diffusion of indigenous information and knowledge. But information gathering is not an end in itself; it should also be processed and routed to the end-user without delay. The challenges of information highways are first and foremost technological.

The nations with the know-how and performing infrastructures for information processing and distribution are undeniably those well ahead of the others. Information highways represent an opportunity for LDCs, and can help compensate for lower levels of technological and economic development. The sectors in the best position to draw a maximum of benefit, and very rapidly, are education, scientific and technical research, medicine, tourism, the valorisation of the cultural heritage and trade and industry.

The rural world, which represents 85 per cent of the population in LDCs, should not be excluded from this process, hence the importance of developing community information systems allowing the codification of all of the information required for the rural sector development by:

— designing interfaces for information access by an illiterate population;

— making such information as civil status data, economic statistics linked to the agricultural sector, handicraft, fishing and cultivation available.

In Senegal, according to the telecentres managers union, the some 10,000 operational telecentres in the country generate an annual turnover of circa 50 million Euros, an activity which, in addition, contributes to the creation of a large number of jobs particularly for young people.

In the light of the analysis of ICTs in the least developed countries and of the identification of the potential needs, it clearly appears that the constraints hindering the development of information and communication of a society are closely linked to the economic and social context and to the different factors belonging to the transfer of technology. Thus, the actual issue to be addressed by a strategy for the promotion of ICTs is that of determining in what way such communication tools as the Internet or the telephone, radio and television can contribute to the local development of communities, thereby creating the conditions of a sustainable development in each of these countries and in the regions which surround them.

The government's role is, first and foremost, to present a vision for the future, a strategy and an environment favourable to the implementation of a national information and communication infrastructure, and to ensure that all sectors are benefiting from it. Its mission should consist in:

— Elaboration of national plans for the adoption of informatics and new communication technologies by government or public bodies, and follow-up on their implementation;

— Promotion of the use of the new information and communication technologies in the civil service in order to improve public services productivity and stimulate information and communication industries;

— Significant support to public establishments, such as higher education bodies and research institutions;

— Creating a framework and procedures for the participation of all sectors in the implementation of a national information and communication infrastructure, the coordination and harmonisation of different actors' efforts, including the private sector, non-governmental organisations and the media.

— Establishing relationships with other countries, international organisations and regional bodies, for coordinated and harmonious development at both the regional and the international levels;

— Designing the legal framework and the required regulations to resolve the problems related to costs of telecommunications and accessibility, universal service objectives, intellectual property, respect for privacy, free circulation of information and the convergence of radio and television broadcasting with telecommunications;

In this respect, governments' principal tasks are listed below:

— *Telecommunications*: the issue is to facilitate the liberalisation of national telecommunications and radio and TV broadcasting public services. In this respect, legislation should be defined and incentive measures for the private sector's collaboration in the implementation of this infrastructure should be offered, and an independent and strong regulatory body in charge of the regulation of partnerships between the public sector and the private sector and, particularly, international participation, should be established.

— *Intellectual Property*: LDCs require a legal framework which can take into balanced consideration intellectual property as an international obligation and the necessity to meet the basic intellectual needs of the poor. Governments should pass and implement copyright legislation and increase public awareness of intellectual property rights. They should also simultaneously forecast and design palliatives in respect of the negative impact of such laws on society.

— *Respect for privacy*: laws for the protection of private persons against any breach of their privacy that could be caused by the new technologies should be adopted.

— *Free circulation of information:* formulation and application of laws and regulations for the protection of the freedom of speech, which represents a guarantee for easy access to information and services.

— Facilitate equal access for women to the new information technologies.

This aims to develop in the private and public sector decision- makers informed decision-makers, allowing them to improve their knowledge of the value of the use of information, national and international information resources, research methods and direct information retrieval on the Internet network or on other international information networks, the electronic mail and "knowledge bases" networks, potential social, economic and cultural effects of the new information and communication systems and the necessity for training in order to adapt structures and work methods in order to benefit from electronic media and spaces. The objective is the introduction of the new ICT in schools and universities.

The government's role should be supported by development cooperation, resulting in the implementation of institutional and regulatory frameworks in order to stimulate a proper use of ICTs in the educational sector. The role of NGOs may range from the articulation of needs which may be increasingly marginalized by technological progress, to the assessment of the population's real information needs, including the supply of relevant data at local level. The private sector can both provide the technical infrastructure and promote the creation of content by means of innovative ideas.

Access to Eelectronic Economy

The digital economy is being shaped not only by the development and diffusion of computer hardware and software, but also by much cheaper and rapidly increasing electronic connectivity. The Internet in particular is helping to level the playing field among large and small firms in business-to-business e-commerce. In the past, larger companies had increasingly used private networks to carry out electronic commerce, but high costs kept the resulting efficiencies out of reach for most small businesses.

Citizens of developed countries have definitively crossed into a new era of economic and social experience bound up in digitally-based technological changes that are producing new ways of working, new means and manners of communicating, new goods and services, and new forms of community. It measures the economic performance of information technology (IT) industries and their substantial impact on growth and inflation, and sketches the emerging dimensions of e-commerce. For the first time, it can be reasonably claimed that the extraordinary dynamism of the IT sector and the new, proliferating forms of e-business and e-commerce are part of an enduring and broad economic pattern.

The rapid pace and proliferation of innovation associated with IT, and the substantial increases in U.S. productivity and growth associated with IT-related innovation, now appear to be persistent. At the core of the proposition that the digital economy can produce higher long-term productivity gains and national growth than we knew in the 1970s and 1980s are certain singular qualities associated with information technologies.

Most obviously, these technologies provide new ways of managing and using a resource that is common to every sector and aspect of economic life; namely information. Compared, for example, to the introduction of refrigeration or jet propulsion, IT innovations can be applied across the economy and throughout the economic process. As a result, economic gains directly associated with improving the capacity to obtain, process and transmit information mount up.

Further, many IT markets exhibit what economists call "network effects": The more the technology is deployed, the greater its value. Compare certain information technologies to automobiles. When you own a car, its value to you is basically the same whether 5,000 or 1 million other people own the same brand of automobile. When you buy a computer operating system or graphics program, its value to you increases as more people buy it, because their purchases of the same program increase your ability to digitally communicate and interact. The spread of IT innovations in the digital economy affect growth in other ways.

For example, IT innovations appear to raise business investment in equipment. The last seven years have seen the fastest growth of business investment in equipment on record, and IT investments have accounted for almost two-thirds of that growth.

The digital economy also can stimulate improvements in workers' skills, since many firms have to train their employees to use information technologies. This may be one reason why Americans across the work force are making real wage gains for the first time in two decades.

Further, IT markets with the network effects described above tend to be dominated by a handful of products and companies, and this tendency creates the possibility of beneficial economies of scale. Perhaps most important of all, a dynamic of cascading or continuous innovation has characterized the development and deployment of information technologies in this period.

Productivity gains come not just from deploying innovative technologies that enable workers to process information faster. In addition, firms intent on taking advantage of innovative new technologies often have to rethink the way they operate and reorganize their operations, which can produce a round of organizational innovation. Many firms also have discovered that the new technologies can be used to develop and produce new goods or services for themselves, producing yet another round of innovation.

Furthermore, as these areas of potential are widely recognized and the process spreads from firm to firm, this generates demand for faster information processing. This can lead to another round of innovation in IT itself—part of the basis for the doubling of chip capacity every 18 months, articulated as Moore's Law—and the cascade can begin again.

A leading example of this dynamic is the Internet itself. Regular and large increases in chip power provided a technological foundation for the Internet, which in turn generated myriad innovations first in software and then in how businesses organize themselves and operate, which in turn has led to more myriad innovations in the goods and services available to businesses and individuals. The complex of hardware and software innovations that encompass the IT sector have made information the most important basis for creating value in the economy. The process of creating value from information, throughout and across the economy, is the ultimate basis for the digital economy.

At the same time, the U.S. economy has enjoyed a remarkable resurgence. Productivity growth, one of the most important indicators of economic health, doubled its pace from a sluggish 1.4-percent average rate between 1973 and 1995, to a 2.8-percent rate from 1995 to 1999. Evidence is increasing that these two phenomena are not coincidental but derive substantially from the same phenomenon: the synergistic convergence of dramatic increases in computer power, an explosion in connectivity, and increasingly powerful new software.

These advances in technology have produced sharp declines in the prices of computer processing, data storage and retrieval, and communications, that are in turn driving both the surge in Internet activity and the increases in business investment in IT hardware and software. Such investment has been a major source of recent U.S. economic strength.

The advances in computer power overwhelm imagination. Technologies associated with computer use, such as data storage technologies, have also shown dramatic improvements in performance and even more dramatic cost reductions.

The capacity of today's hard- disk drives is doubling every nine months and the average price per megabyte for hard-disk drives has declined from $11.54 in 1988 to an estimated $.02 in 1999. As a consequence of technological advances in microprocessors, storage, and other components, already steep annual declines in computer costs from 1987 to 1994 accelerated sharply beginning in 1995. Similar improvements have occurred in communications technologies.For example, wavelength division multiplexing, digital subscriber lines, and cable modems have produced exponential increases in the speed of data communication and the carrying capacity of the communications infrastructure. The carrying capacity of fiber is currently doubling every 12 months.

Between 1994 and 1998, the price of telecommunications equipment declined by 2 percent per year. Price declines for computers and peripheral equipment and for communications equipment have spurred major increases in business IT investment and extraordinary growth in U.S. production of computers, communications equipment and semiconductors. In addition, the declining costs of computing and communications are helping to drive complementary investment in new software that harnesses and further enhances the productive capacity of IT hardware and infrastructure. The new economy is being shaped by developments not only in computer hardware and software, but also in electronic connectivity.

Larger businesses have been increasing efficiencies through standardizing and automating routine transactions electronically for some time. Until recently, however, most small and medium sized businesses found that the costs of necessary hardware, software, and communications service for these systems exceeded the benefits. The advent of the Internet as an instrument of commerce fundamentally altered this equation by cutting the costs of software and communications services needed to conduct electronic transactions.

Beginning in the mid-1990s, as a result of the convergence toward digital formats and the development of de facto standards for digital networks, such as the Internet's technical specifications, the expansion and commercialization of the Internet made connecting computers and communications devices easier and cheaper.

Commercial opportunities on the Internet and the falling costs of computer and communications hardware created an extraordinarily fertile environment for innovations that are creating new value and new efficiencies for businesses of all sizes. The Internet is both an effect and a cause of the new economy. It is, in part, a product of the powerful technological and economic changes that are shaping a new epoch of economic experience. Networks, like telephone networks or the Internet, are subject to a phenomenon called "network effects" or "network externalities." Establishing a network involves large, up-front fixed costs, but adding an additional user to an existing network costs very little.

Conversely, the value of a network to participants is low when the number of participants on the network is low, but rises rapidly as network participation expands.

For example, a network of a single telephone is of no use. Adding another telephone increases the value of the network because now calls can be made between the two phones. As phones are added, the number of possible connections rises almost as fast as the number of phones squared. Similarly, as the number of people online has grown, so has the value of being online to each Internet user.

Moreover, as the Internet gains popularity, its technological specifications have become a default standard, encouraging new hardware and software innovations that use Internet technology as a platform. Fundamental engineering breakthroughs alone do not have important economic effects until their costs and applications become favorable.

For example, by the mid-1970s, Xerox PARC had already made several breakthroughs underpinning today's IT revolution: a microcomputer with a mouse, graphical user interface, and Ethernet communications capabilities.

But there was no mass market for their machine, which at the time cost about $25,000 each to produce, especially given its slower processing speed and the absence of applications software that drives computer use today. In contrast, technological advances in recent years have brought IT costs down to a far more commercially attractive range, and new software applications for networked systems have been developed.

Nothing approaching the activities now conducted over the Internet was possible a few years ago. Push back the technology or cost declines in any one of the four elements--computer processing, data storage, software, or communications—just a few years and the Internet activities we now view as commonplace would be too frustrating or too costly for a mass market.

Likewise, roll back any one of those elements and business would have found IT investment to be far less productive. As applications software is developed to exploit the continuing plunge in hardware prices in coming years, businesses and consumers will find new ways to create value and increase efficiency.

Impact of E-Commerce

The U.S. economy coincides with the growing use of the Internet, including the rapid growth of electronic commerce. In ever greater numbers, people are shopping, looking for jobs, and researching medical problems online. Businesses are moving their supply networks online, participating in and developing online marketplaces, and expanding their use of networked systems to improve a host of business processes. And new products and services are being created and integrated into the networked world.

Over the past year, Internet access in the United States and Canada grew by more than 40 percent; over the same period, Internet access in all other parts of the world more than doubled. Consumers today--wherever they are in the world--go online to shop, learn about different products and providers, search for jobs, manage their finances, obtain health information and scan their hometown newspapers.

While many of these activities are not captured by official output and productivity measures, a growing body of anecdotal evidence suggests that the digital revolution is improving many people's lives. Individuals with Internet access increasingly approach the Web as a market space. People online do research before they buy, make purchase commitments, arrange financing, take delivery of digital products, and obtain followup service. The "commerce" in e-commerce encompasses all of these activities.

However, when measuring business-to-consumer (B2C) e-commerce in particular, it is the commitment to purchase--the transactional component--that both buyers and sellers can easily identify and quantify. This transactional component is the focus of most current e-commerce measurements. In March 2000, the U.S. Bureau of the Census released the first official measure of e-retail, an important subset of business-to-consumer e-commerce. By contrast, private estimates for consumer e-commerce in the fourth quarter of 1999 ranged from approximately $4 billion to $14 billion.

However, many private estimates of B2C e-commerce include the value of a wide range of consumer online purchases such as airline tickets, hotel rooms, and shares of stocks that are not captured in The Census Bureau's survey of retail establishments. When these private estimates are adjusted to cover only those purchases included in the retail measure, the Census Bureau estimate of $5.3 billion appears to fall in the midrange.

Private surveys conducted shortly after the holiday season indicated that such problems were minimal and that online customer satisfaction was high. Nonetheless, some analysts believe that delivering goods ordered by consumers from e-retailers will prove to be more costly and complex than currently appreciated. The ultimate size of online consumer sales will depend on resolving these fulfillment issues, along with other important matters such as taxation, consumer protection, privacy, intellectual property rights, security, and network reliability. In the consumer realm, the most significant impact of e-commerce may be on the pricing of goods and services.

Potential buyers can check the price and availability of products from a variety of sites in far less time than it would take to conduct store-to-store comparisons in the world of bricks and mortar. Furthermore, online digital shopping spaces can be perused for consumers by software specialized to operate as digital shoppers. Such digital agents, known as "bots," cruise through numbers of Internet sites almost instantaneously, searching for the most favorable price and feature combinations. One would expect that this ability to easily and cheaply gather information on prices and product characteristics would force Internet retailers to charge the same low price--one that would approach their cost--on the same or comparable products. One might also expect these online prices to influence prices charged in physical stores. Thus far, however, the data on these matters are mixed.

Live auctions have existed for a long time, but their practical uses have been limited by the expense and difficulty of getting prospective buyers to a single location at the same time. Sealed bid auctions are less expensive, but they often do not produce the highest possible return to the seller. By contrast, the Internet provides a relatively low-cost and convenient way of bringing buyers and sellers together, and the use of auction sites such as eBay has grown rapidly.

A "single price" model holds for most offline goods and services since most offline sellers do not have sufficient information to vary their prices from customer-to-customer and because changing the price of individually tagged items may involve considerable cost. Where providers do have sufficient customer information and price adjustments are relatively easy to make, however, variable pricing can produce benefits to both seller and consumer.

For example, airlines have long set lower fares for tickets issued 21 days in advance that include a Saturday night stay and much higher fares for next-day tickets. More recently, airlines have developed an e-mail strategy to attract "spur of the moment" travelers with last minute travel deals. As a result, while vacation travelers obtain fares at a lower cost than if the airline charged a single price for all seats on the plane, business travelers can be confident that they can secure seats with little advanced notice, and airlines operate with a higher proportion of their seats filled.

The Internet opens up this airline-type variable pricing to many other types of goods and services, creating the potential for greater specificity in variable pricing. By gauging the price sensitivity of particular consumers relative to the marginal cost of the good and its availability, online sellers can fine tune prices for individual customers to maximize profits. Manufacturers, retailers, and online magazines now offer detailed product, warranty, and repair information, along with comparisons of competitive products. Rather than comparison shopping at brick-and-mortar stores, consumers can now get reliable information conveniently on the Web.

Consumers cannot test drive an automobile on the Web, so auto buyers still want to visit car dealerships. However, consumers who do their homework online can approach dealers with a wealth of information that can strengthen their bargaining position and reduce some of the stress of car buying.

The Internet increases the ability of patients to participate more actively in matters related to their own health. A study by the California HealthCare Foundation cites estimates that the Internet offers at least 17,000 different health care sites and that some 24.8 million U.S. adults have searched for health information. This number is projected to grow to over 30 million during 2000. Jupiter Communications has estimated that 45 percent of online consumers access the Internet for health information. Today, some patients arrive at their doctors' offices carrying possible diagnoses downloaded from sites such as Healtheon/WebMD or America Online Health Channel.

In addition, people with Internet access can obtain information about their healthcare plans, find doctors, and in some cases submit claims for fee reimbursement. Doctors, too, are increasing their use of the Internet as a source of information on the latest news in medical research. Other aspects of health care delivery, including laboratory results reporting, prescriptions, office visit scheduling, and records transmittal may move online once issues such as privacy and authentication are resolved.

Many private companies now post job openings on their company's Web site, and in some cases these sites can accept online applications. Web site recruiting among the North American-based Global 500 was even more prevalent, with over 90 percent of such firms participating and 71 percent accepting applications online. In addition to firm-specific online recruiting, a growing number of Web sites offer online employment classifieds, grouping together requests from multiple employers.

Some of these sites are maintained by newspaper companies, traditional providers of employment classifieds. Others have been established to specialize in specific employment areas. Some observers believe that effective online recruiting faces substantial barriers. The Internet's original purpose was to disseminate research and information, and this use continues to be important today.

Educational research and technical materials are available online to students, researchers, scientists, and engineers anywhere in the world. Many universities make their research papers available on the Internet, and most academic and professional journals are available online. In addition, previously unpublished information is increasingly available on the Internet. For example, students can download lectures at their convenience, and live classroom presentations are broadcast on the Internet with students submitting questions via e-mail. The Internet also provides access to research of a more general or recreational nature.

News with frequent updates is available from local, national, and foreign sources, as are weather and traffic information. Numerous online services also provide information covering everything from the floor plans of museums and restaurant reviews, to local television and radio listings. During several recent foreign conflicts and natural disasters, the Internet played a role in providing news and information when traditional media outlets were closed.

Federal, state and local governments also are rapidly developing new ways of using the Internet to communicate with clients and to provide public services to businesses and individuals. Many state and local governments are also moving services online. Interested individuals and businesses can find information on a wide variety of topics such as registration, parks, and trash removal. The spread of Internet access is being accompanied by a proliferation of new community spaces online.

Some of these are commercial spaces such as online auctions that allow consumers to sell or trade goods and services. Others are meeting spaces where individuals interact around a particular interest or topic--from chat rooms for hobbyists, and online current events discussions, to support groups for people facing similar challenges. In the process of providing places for individuals to interact, these online spaces create virtual communities.

Digital Business

Business-to-consumer e-commerce is the most visible aspect of e-commerce, it is only a small part of what is now possible due to recent technological advances. Increasingly, business-to-business (B2B) e-commerce is emerging as an area of critical importance for businesses faced with rapidly changing markets and opportunities.

Transactions between businesses account for the lion's share of commercial activity, and e-commerce technologies appear to have an enormous potential to make these transactions more efficient. Companies are also using these technologies to increase the efficiency of their internal operations. One important difference is the degree to which non-Internet network transactions, such as those conducted over electronic data interchange (EDI) systems, are included in the estimates of B2B e-commerce.

Irrespective of the dollar amounts, the market researchers all expect strong growth as companies seek to cut costs and increase efficiency by streamlining their purchasing, sales, and other business processes. At present, many firms are at the beginning stages of implementing e-commerce technologies in their business processes. A recent National Association of Manufacturers survey found that 68 percent of manufacturers are not yet using electronic commerce to conduct business transactions.

A Purchasing Magazine survey shows that 38 percent of buyers currently use the Web to conduct at least some of their company's transactions. The survey also finds that of those who do not currently conduct transactions over the Internet, approximately 35 percent say they will begin to conduct transactions electronically within the next year and 54 percent say they will do so within the next three years. Only 11 percent of those not currently online have no expectation of using the Internet for procurement. The potential of e-commerce technologies to transform business practices is evident in the new marketplaces that are developing online.

These important intermediaries have emerged rapidly in virtually all industries, providing new places for buyers and sellers to meet, allowing a variety of pricing schemes to flourish, altering the roles of traditional intermediaries, enabling complex transactions, and, by making vast amounts of information available at very low costs, shifting the balance of power among market participants. E-Bay, for example, which started out providing a marketplace for consumers selling to other consumers (C2C) in online auctions, has expanded to include B2C and B2B transactions.

While the large buyers organizing these online marketplaces hope to achieve significant cost savings, it is difficult to gauge a priori the impact these new arrangements may have on their supply communities. Some suppliers and potential suppliers that had been unable to justify the cost of EDI connections may be much more willing to use the Internet to bid on work that they would otherwise have missed. Concerns have been raised, however, about the potential for these large players to use these markets to reduce competition.

The overall impact will depend on the extent to which actual efficiencies can be achieved as opposed to squeezing supplier margins. One probable side effect of moving these supply networks to the Internet will be to increase the level of investment in Internet technologies. E-commerce technologies also appear to be driving changes among traditional intermediaries—i.e., firms such as wholesalers, travel agents, or shippers, that add value between the production of a good or service and its sale to the final consumer.

Early predictions were that the Internet and e-commerce would create efficiencies by eliminating the need for intermediaries. Manufacturers and service providers would begin selling directly to the customer and "middlemen" would disappear. However, the early speculation failed to appreciate the important role that intermediaries play or the resourcefulness some intermediaries would exhibit in finding new ways to add value in an online world. Instead of vanishing, traditional intermediaries are adapting to exploit new possibilities as providers of logistical, financial, and information services. Internet-based market spaces also broaden market participation by decreasing the costs of participating in B2B markets.

For decades, large companies have used EDI to automate routine paperwork surrounding business transactions, to manage arrangements such as automatic inventory replenishment, and to make purchases according to pre-established terms. Until recently, the use of this e-business activity was limited to large volume supplier/customer relationships because EDI required a fairly sizable investment in dedicated hardware and proprietary software and use of expensive leased telecommunications lines.

As costs of computing power, memory, and storage declined throughout the 1990s, the size threshold at which EDI became cost-effective also declined, but still remained too high for many trading applications. Now, however, the Internet with its open nonproprietary protocols and global reach has emerged as a platform for spreading the efficiencies achievable through the automation of business processes to firms of all sizes. The bulk of B2B e-commerce remains EDI-based, although analysts are predicting that most of the future growth of B2B e-commerce will be Internet-based.

The National Association of Manufacturers estimates that among businesses that currently use the Web for business, 17 percent are using it in place of EDI. The Boston Consulting Group estimates that 86 percent of the

$671 billion in B2B e-commerce in 1998 was EDI conducted over private networks. However, they estimate that the EDI component will fall to 28 percent by 2003. In addition, businesses and even governments have discovered the potential of the Internet as an auction space.

Businesses are using auctions to sell off surplus goods, dispose of used equipment, and post requests for purchase. Business purchasers are also using online auctions to request bids. Owens Corning used an online reverse auction run by Freemarkets, an online auction company, to put bids out for corrugated packaging materials for its 21 U.S. plants. At the end of the day the company had 17 two-year contracts with corrugated packaging material suppliers and had saved an estimated 10 percent.

E-commerce transactions represent only one way in which innovations in computers and communications can add value and make business processes more productive. All business processes have some information component. Specifications for a design must be shared between architects and engineers. The latest maintenance information must be delivered to the mechanic working on the airplane.

The manufacturer of auto interiors needs to know how many blue interiors must be delivered for a manufacturing run at the auto plant. All of these processes benefit when information flows faster, more accurately, and in greater detail to the people who need it. Many companies are experimenting with processes that enable them to share information over a network or the Internet.

For example, BOC Gases replaced a slower, more costly certification procedure with a process that sends product certification results over the Internet for customers that need specialized gas products. Businesses are also using networking technologies to improve processes, such as design and engineering, reducing development time, simplifying manufacturing processes, and integrating design processes. Using Internet technologies to coordinate product design.

A semiconductor producer, has created Web-enabled tools for its new product development process. The company's 2,000 engineers use a standard Web browser to access the company's portfolio of projects and obtain information on phase of development, team composition, deliverables, and time frame. Using communications networks to improve human resource functions.

Using wireless networks to manage inventory more efficiently. Cablevision, a telecommunications and entertainment company, uses wireless mobile computer appliances over a local area network to process inventory transactions in real time, at the point of activity. Using the Internet to provide customer services and answer frequently asked questions.

Many companies are using their company Web site to offer customer services and product information. Ford offers product information and links to dealers, and their "Owner Connection" Web page provides Ford car owners with maintenance information, safety tips, service reminders, do-it-yourself pointers, and online manuals.

Using the Internet to reduce project administration and management costs. Not only are individuals, businesses, and other organizations going online in increasing numbers, but the products and services used in everyday life are becoming increasingly integrated into the networked economy.

The Internet provides a new way to have goods and services delivered. Music, legal advice, software, opera tickets, news reports, books, photographs, movies, and product designs—can all be downloaded directly into a computer. The most dramatic growth in direct, digital download sales will probably be in the music sector, where such sales could rise from 0.1 percent of online sales in 1999 to 25 percent in 2004, followed by software and books. Digitalization is also changing the design of products, so these products can be networked.

For example, home-electronics producers have joined together to develop Home Audio Video Interoperability (HAVi), an open, consumer-electronics-industry standard that will allow digital audio and video devices from different vendors to work together when connected to a network in the consumer's home. Appliances that can be networked are beginning to emerge in other areas as well. New home electronics and appliances will not only be networkable, many of them also will be "network appliances"--that is, appliances that can access the Internet. The television has long been viewed as a potential portal for Internet access.

More recently, simple, low cost dedicated Internet access devices have been introduced. In addition, connectivity is increasingly being viewed as an important feature to add to existing products. At recent trade shows, for example, home appliance manufacturers have unveiled prototype Internet-enabled refrigerators and ovens that offer features such as e-mail, calendar management, automated grocery ordering, and tracking of the service requirements of the appliance.

The development of new technology is still limited by slow connection and transmission speeds and the lack of standards to facilitate individual appliances communicating with one another. As these limitations are addressed, however, the developmental pace of digital products is likely to increase. New technologies that exploit the potential of wireless connections are already creating new ways of communicating and conducting business, reconfiguring many traditional industry and product definitions.

As Internet access migrates from the desktop computer to a range of products, the lines that now separate the transmission of voice, data, and pictures will disappear. New devices under development today will combine cellular telephone, geopositioning, and Internet access in a handheld or automobile device. The technologies that make the digital economy possible are still evolving, as is the environment in which these technologies are being used. Many businesses and individuals remain hesitant about e-commerce because the business environment online does not yet have the same predictability and reliability as it does offline. And the medium itself offers new challenges.

IT and Industries

Information Technology (IT) producing industries—the firms that supply the goods and services that support IT-enabled business practices across the economy, as well as the Internet and e-commerce. Over the past decade, and especially since the mid-1990s, these industries have been a powerful factor in the economy's rapid and sustained growth, a significant restraint on inflation, and a focal point of prolific technological innovation. Since the mid-1990s, IT-producing industries have shown extraordinary dynamism. Prepackaged software and computer services had the highest growth rate, increasing their output.

Over the same period, the computer hardware and communications equipment industries increased their output at a 9 percent annual rate, and output in the communications services sector rose at a 7 percent annual pace. The rapid increase in these industries' share of the economy after 1994 is particularly impressive in view of both the rapid growth of the economy as a whole and the accelerated decline in IT prices over the period.

A modest share of IT growth also reflected spending related to addressing Y2K-related computer problems. ESA analysts have estimated that Y2K-related spending accounted for roughly 7 percent of the output of IT-producing industries in 1998 and 1999. The declining prices of IT goods and services have worked, directly and indirectly, to reduce overall inflation in the U.S. economy. Over the same period, lower prices in the IT sector reduced overall U.S. inflation directly, on average, by about 0.5 percentage points a year--from 2.3 percent to 1.8 percent.

IT equipment, including software, plays in business investment activity. In current dollars, industry spending on IT equipment and software rose from $198 billion in 1992, or 44 percent of all equipment spending, to $407 billion in 1999, or 46 percent. Over the same period, "other capital equipment," including industrial equipment, fell from 38 percent of total equipment and software investment spending to 32 percent, and transportation equipment ranged between 18 percent and

21 percent. Because prices for IT equipment and software have been falling, investment spending shifts are even more pronounced when expressed in real dollars, rather than nominal amounts.

Since 1995, prices of IT capital equipment and software have dropped by an average 6.7 percent per year, while prices for transportation capital equipment have increased at a 0.6-percent average annual rate and prices for other types of capital equipment have increased at a 1.5-percent rate. As a result, real business investment spending on IT equipment and software more than doubled between 1995 and 1999, from $243 billion to $510 billion, while real spending on transportation equipment increased by about half and real spending on other capital equipment increased slightly.

Over the decade of the 1990s, growing industry spending on IT equipment and software was a significant factor in the high rate of growth of U.S. spending on all categories of equipment to 9-to-10 percent per year, compared to 5-to-6 percent a year in the 1980s. In 1999, business spending for IT equipment and software represented more than three-fourths of the 12 percent real growth in total equipment and software spending that year, compared to 65 percent of the real growth in equipment spending for 1995-1998 and less than 50 percent for 1993-1994.

Despite the rapid decline in computer prices, computers' share of IT equipment investment in nominal dollars remained relatively constant over the 1992-1999 period. Other IT equipment, including spending on communications equipment, remained the largest category of IT equipment purchases, although its share declined from 47 percent in 1992 to 41 percent in 1999.

Analysis of the composition of IT investment in real rather than nominal dollars yields a somewhat different picture because prices have declined far more rapidly for computer than for other kinds of IT equipment and software.

Measured in real dollars, beginning in 1994, investment in computers accelerated more rapidly than investment in the two other IT categories, surpassing investment in these categories by 1998. In 1999, price-adjusted spending for computers totaled $222 billion, compared with $149 billion for software and $170 billion for other IT equipment. The surge in IT investment since 1994 has been accompanied by sharp increases in R&D investment in the economy as a whole and in IT-producing industries in particular. Growth in IT industries' share of private R&D is largely the result of increased R&D investment by manufacturers of electronic components and software.

In the computer industry, annual R&D investment dropped from an average $11 billion during 1990-92, to $5 billion during 1993-95, then rose to $10 billion during 1996-98. One reason for this lack of overall growth may be that as computer demand has shifted toward micro-computers, more computer-related R&D has shifted to component manufacturers and software firms.

Impact of IT on Labour Productivity

Today, U.S. productivity pattern, in which productivity gains have strengthened as the expansion has matured, is unprecedented for the postwar period. In previous postwar expansions, productivity growth has slowed as the expansion enters its mature phase. One reason for the extraordinary pattern of productivity in the current expansion appears to be the rapid growth in the real net stock of IT capital per labor hour, especially computer hardware.

This rapid growth of real net IT capital created significant IT "capital deepening," beginning in 1991 and accelerating sharply after 1995. The ratio of the capital stock of computer hardware to hours worked increased, on average, by 16.3 percent per year over the period 1991-95, and 33.7 percent per year during 1996-99. Capital deepening in computer software also grew at double-digit rates during both periods, while the growth rate in communications equipment increased from 2.4 to 5.0 percent. A major factor behind IT capital deepening has been the falling prices of IT, especially computer hardware, reflecting rapid and continuous improvements in quality.

Multifactor productivity (MFP) growth reflects the impact of factors in addition to quality-adjusted capital and labor inputs--for example, technical changes not directly incorporated in capital and labor, organizational improvements, and economies of scale. All categories of IT capital contribute disproportionately to labor productivity growth, compared to their shares of the total private nonfarm business sector and their shares of the total net capital stock.

However, the contribution of computer hardware to productivity growth has been extraordinarily large. A research indicates that during the years 1996-99, computer hardware deepening accounted for 24 percent of all labor productivity growth. The size of this contribution is especially remarkable because computers constitute just 1.8 percent of the private nonfarm business sector and less than 1 percent of overall capital stock. The reason that IT, with such a small share of the economy and of the total capital stock, has contributed so powerfully to productivity growth is that the rapidly growing IT investments have been unusually productive.

Market conditions dictate that business investments in computer hardware must earn very high rates of return. For one thing, the rapid and continuous improvements in IT quality mean that existing computer hardware becomes obsolete and hence depreciates very quickly. In addition, sharply falling hardware prices mean that businesses investing in IT equipment face rapid capital losses as purchased equipment quickly loses market value. Economists who held until recently that the impact of computers on U.S. productivity could be a transitory effect of unusually favorable economic circumstances have begun to credit IT for dramatic increases in the trend growth rates of U.S. output and productivity since 1995.

One reason for this change in view has been the increasing attention paid by researchers to the productivity effects of software and communications equipment, in addition to computer hardware.

The Congressional Budget Office talks about "computers," distinguishing between computer "use" and computer "production", while the Economic Report of the President refers to "computers and software." Jorgenson and Stiroh include in IT "capital services" those from computer, software, and communications capital. There are factors contributing to labor productivity growth acceleration other than capital deepening and technical advance that are intended to highlight IT's contribution to the acceleration of labor productivity growth.

Since IT investments improve productivity, those industries making the most intensive use of IT should show higher productivity growth than industries that use IT less intensively. Evidence of such a pattern at the industry level, however, remains mixed.

IT-producing industries have recorded astonishingly high productivity gains and have been a dominant force in aggregate U.S. productivity growth. Furthermore, outside the IT-producing sector itself, goods-producing industries that are IT intensive have achieved higher productivity gains than their counterparts that have not invested heavily in IT.

However, official output measures for IT-intensive service industries do not indicate significant productivity gains. Indeed, between 1990 and 1997, despite heavy investments in IT and a three-decade buildup of the real net IT capital stock, IT-using service industries as a group recorded declining productivity. The significant multifactor productivity growth in IT-producing industries, improved labor productivity growth in both IT-producing and IT-using goods industries, and alternative views of IT's effect on productivity in service industries.

A study found strong labor productivity, as well as multifactor productivity gains in the computer-producing sector, implying that this sector positively contributes to overall productivity growth. IT-using service industries actually showed a negative growth rate of 0.3 percent a year, compared to 1.3 percent annual productivity gains by non-IT intensive service industries. These results largely reflect the difficult problems in conceptualizing and measuring output in many service industries. In view of these measurement problems, we compared growth in GPO/W of IT-using service industries with that of the non-IT intensive service industries, but excluding 10 hard-to-measureservice industries.

IT-using service industries show slightly greater GPO/W growth than non-IT intensive service industries, and the overall annual average GPO/W growth for 1990-97 rises from 1.38 percent to 2.34 percent. Because hard-to-measure service industries together account for 44 percent of the total GPO by IT-using service industries, the effect of IT on service industry productivity will remain clouded until development of better output measures.

Like the macroeconomic studies, recent firm-level analyses show that IT contributes substantially to productivity growth. This contribution is especially strong where businesses undertake organizational and other changes that complement the adoption of IT. In one study, analyzed firms in four groups based on their levels of IT investment and degree of decentralization. While they found that average productivity was highest among firms that were high in both IT investment and decentralized organization, they also found that productivity was lowest among those firms that were high in IT investment but low in decentralization.

IT Workers

Information technology workers produce and maintain the knowledge, ideas and information critical to the development of the digital economy. Demand for IT workers has increased with the spread of networked computers, the Internet, e-commerce, and the associated growing demand for high-quality digitized products and services. Moreover, the demand for IT workers is increasingly focused on more highly-skilled and highly paid people, as the rapid pace of innovation rewards high skills and technology reduces the number of less-skilled and lower paid IT jobs. In 1998, the IT workforce--covering workers in IT-producing industries and workers in IT occupations in other industries-- totaled roughly 7.4 million workers, or 6.1 percent of all workers.

While IT employment has grown faster than overall employment for many years, the growth in both IT-producing industries and IT occupations accelerated in the mid-1990s. IT industry employment grew almost 28 percent from 1994 to 1998, and employment in IT occupations increased by 22 percent over the same period. By contrast, over those same years, total U.S. nonfarm employment rose by about 11 percent.

Jobs in IT-producing firms, after growing more slowly than overall employment in 1993 and 1994, increased dramatically in 1995 and thereafter, growing at an average annual rate of 6.5 percent. The number of workers in IT-producing firms grew from 3.9 million in 1992 to 5.2 million workers in 1998. Even at this level, employment in IT-producing firms in 1998 accounted for less than 5 percent of total private employment. The overall growth in IT-producing industry employment masks a churning of IT jobs, with significant job increases in some areas and significant declines in others. Many information technologies have short life cycles, and employers intent on quickly getting a product or service to market often prefer to hire workers skilled in new technologies rather than retrain their current workers.

Computing and communications technologies have lowered barriers to entry, especially to markets that provide information technology and other services. These technologies provide small businesses with size and resource advantages usually available to larger, established companies. By using the Internet, they can compete outside of local markets, even in global markets. The same technologies allow foreign companies greater access to U.S. markets. More players in the market means more job churning as there will be winners and losers. Employment in IT-producing industries is also affected by the increasing use of outsourcing to other industries. Among workers in all IT-producing industries, those in software and computer services industries, including computer programming services and software development, earned the highest average wage of $65,300 in 1998. These industries paid wages that were higher than the total private industry average wage in 1998, and almost all of them had higher than average annual wage growth from 1992 to 1998.

The broadest definition would recognize that, as the economy becomes more digitized, most occupations will involve the manufacture or operation of equipment that includes forms of information technology, such as a computer chip. A more narrow definition might include only the "core" IT occupations of computer scientists, computer engineers, systems analysts and computer programmers; these are the IT positions that require the most education and skills, are the highest paid, and are in greatest demand.

There are number of highly-skilled IT workers, or IT workers in occupations that generally require at least an associate degree, increased from 2.2 million in 1992 to 3.2 million in 1998. The fastest growth occurred among those with the highest skills - core IT occupations - who increased their share of total IT employment from 28 percent to 41 percent. Between 1994 and 1998, total high-skilled IT employment increased 35 percent, more than three times as much as the national average, and core IT occupations grew more than five times faster than all other jobs.

By contrast, employment in lower-skilled IT occupations, such as computer operators, communications equipment operators and billing and posting clerks, declined from 926,000 to 852,000, or 9 percent. During the same period, employment among moderately-skilled IT workers, including telephone and electronic equipment installers, assemblers and repairers, grew somewhat more slowly than the national average. Private surveys and interviews with Chief Information Officers provide additional insight into the specific IT skills in greatest demand.

The growth in e-commerce, for example, has increased demand for workers with Internet-related technical skills, including network specialists, help desk/ end user support staff and Internet/intranet developers. E-commerce growth has also increased the demand for workers with a knowledge of sales, marketing and business planning.

Many IT workers that used to work in back offices are now required to learn how to deal with customers and convince them to make online purchases. In addition, as more firms outsource for IT services, demand has increased for project managers and people who can negotiate and manage vendor contracts. Earnings in IT occupations also vary by geographic location and company size, as they do for many other industries.

In America, Bureau of Labor Statistics examined the available national employment and wage data for core IT occupations over the period 1992 to 1997. They reasoned that an imbalance should produce above-average growth in both employment and wages, and below-average unemployment rates. BLS found that while the unemployment rates for core IT occupations were consistently lower than the national average for this period, employment and wage growth had not been consistently above average for all core IT occupations.

IT and Trade

US's IT companies are powerful competitors in markets around the world. Yet the United States ran a trade deficit in information technology goods of almost $66 billion in 1999. In 1997, a study shows that when the United States exported $121.4 billion of IT goods and services, foreign sales by overseas IT affiliates of American companies totaled $196 billion. In the same year, American-based IT affiliates of foreign companies reported U.S. sales totaling $110.5 billion. Over the same period, U.S. imports of IT goods increased at an average rate of 12.3 percent a year. In fact, the United States has run trade deficits since 1983 in many categories of IT hardware, including semiconductors, household audio and video equipment, and computer storage devices. The negative balance of payments on cross-border sales of telecommunications services is a reflection of calling patterns and differences in national telecommunications rates. More international calls originate here than in other countries because of the strong U.S. economy, relatively high U.S. income levels, and large immigrant populations in this country. In addition, because American markets are more open and competitive, foreign callers pay less to U.S. carriers to complete calls to the United States than Americans pay to foreign carriers to complete calls going the other way. Many U.S. IT firms, spurred by competition from low-cost foreign producers and the liberalization by a growing number of countries of controls on direct investment and capital flows, have moved lower value-added production overseas.

As a result, intra-firm trade, defined as cross-border sales between parents and affiliates of U.S. and foreign multinational companies, accounts for a significant portion of the trade in IT products. In 1997, for instance, U.S. exports to affiliated firms in core IT hardware industries--computer and office equipment; electronic components and accessories; and audio, video and communications equipment--amounted to roughly 60 percent of U.S. exports of goods in these classes of IT hardware. Trade between U.S. parent companies and their overseas affiliates has contributed to a reduction in the size of the U.S. trade deficit in information technology products.

The global competitiveness of the U.S. IT industry is apparent in the comparison of sales by U.S. IT affiliates abroad with sales by foreign-owned IT affiliates stationed in the United States. In 1997, for example, foreign sales by U.S.-owned overseas affiliates in the computer and office equipment industry exceeded sales in this country by foreign-owned U.S. affiliates in the same industry by $67 billion. Similarly, the balance of sales in 1997 favored American-owned foreign providers of computer processing and information retrieval services by $41 billion and U.S.-owned foreign producers in the electronic components and accessories industry by $20 billion.

The information technology sector has played a critical role in the economic success of recent years. Businesses across the economy have been investing heavily in IT hardware and software to harness the potential created by falling prices and by the increasing capacities of computer processing, storage media and communications links.

Business strategies and even the structures of companies and industries are being transformed as communication within companies and among the members of corporate alliances occurs more rapidly, with more customized information, and with greater security, interactivity, and timeliness than before. The same quality of communication that once was limited to a narrow group of close contacts can now be extended to a much wider "reach" of contacts. The IT revolution is affecting everyone's life.

The advances and spread of IT are part of the reason why we now have the lowest unemployment rate and fastest growth in real wages in three decades and the longest expansion on record. Consumers are making a small but increasing amount of their purchases online and using the Internet to make more informed purchases offline. IT is also transforming the way most firms operate. As employers substitute IT for labor, workers have to develop new skills.

The hallmark of the New Economy is higher sustainable growth due to faster improvement in labor productivity. IT can support higher rates of labor productivity gains and output growth, so long as IT innovation and price declines persist, and non-IT industries continue to invest heavily in IT products and services.

Both of these conditions are expected to persist into the future. Experts in the semiconductor, computer, storage, and communications industries have expressed confidence that rapid rates of product innovation and price decline can continue for at least another decade. Experts in non-IT industries also have expressed confidence in their capacity to benefit enormously from further substantial investments in IT. The prospect of healthier productivity gains over both a medium term and a longer run has significant implications for the future standard of living and a range of fiscal issues facing government at all levels.

For example, faster productivity growth translates into more tax revenue, which in turns creates larger budget surpluses and longer positive balances for trust funds such as those for Social Security and Medicare. Faster productivity growth also means lower inflation, reducing the additional costs of COLAs for most entitlement programs.

In most industries, IT investments do not expand capacity; rather, they provide general cost savings, reduce errors, provide the basis for more prompt and informed decisions, and increase customer satisfaction. For industries in which IT investments directly expand capacity to provide services a slowdown in demand should directly slow IT investment. Because IT investments are commonly driven by pressures to keep pace with competitors, in terms of costs and satisfying customer demand for more responsive products, IT investment should weather a slowdown in demand better than capacity expanding investments. The spread of IT could also moderate the sharp declines in manufacturing inventories that occur in recessions.

By improving communications with suppliers and customers, IT has facilitated manufacturers' efforts to limit their inventory exposure. If U.S. manufacturers of durable goods today held inventories at the 1988 inventory to sales ratio, they would be holding an additional $115 billion in inventory. The cost savings from reduced inventories takes several forms. First, there is the average savings of about $10 billion a year from not having to pay to accumulate as much new inventory in each of the eleven years. Second, the cumulative $115 billion in funds that would have been spent for inventory have been used to invest elsewhere or pay down debt. By this point, the financial benefit of the second effect exceeds the benefit from the first. Third, the companies are spared the expense of storing and securing one-third more inventory than they now hold. Fourth, they avoid the inevitable losses from holding inventories for products that lose favor in the marketplace.

Today's leaner inventories should, other things equal, cushion the depth of the next recession by narrowing the gap between declines in output and demand. The U.S. labor productivity boom of the last four years has outpaced not only its own performance from 1973 to 1995, but also the labor productivity gains of other major industrial countries in recent years. The U.S. macroeconomic environment since the early 1990s has stimulated an investment boom. Both fiscal and monetary policy have contributed. The 1990s began with very large budget deficits projected to grow even larger. However, prudent policies to curb spending and raise revenues were introduced, and the fiscal picture has reversed. Sound macroeconomic policies have helped lower unemployment and inflation, but they cannot account for the recent multi-year doubling of labor productivity growth. For that, look to more technologically based explanations. For example, there is the view that fundamental technological changes, from electricity to IT, take a very long time to generate labor productivity breakthroughs - and when they do, labor productivity rises very sharply.

Another important issue concerning the dynamics of the New Economy is their effect on jobs. In an aggregate or macroeconomic sense, the New Economy has been characterized by strong job and wage growth. With lower inflation and accommodating monetary policy, unemployment has fallen below 4 percent, the lowest rate since 1969.

The unemployment rate of those with less education and experience has fallen along with the rates of everyone else, although it remains higher than those of better educated and experienced workers. Similarly, with everyone else, workers near the bottom of the ladder in recent years have enjoyed strong real wage growth.

The number of well-paid jobs in the IT producing and IT-using sectors is growing rapidly, even as the number of lower-paid IT-related jobs is shrinking. It is reasonable to assume that IT, by raising labor productivity, must displace jobs somewhere in the economy. However, there is no clear evidence about what types of jobs are displaced most rapidly by IT. A significant percentage of jobs in modern America involve collecting and/or processing information, and/or making decisions based on information; but some sectors, such as education and financial services, have a higher proportion of information-intensive jobs than other sectors.

Measures of the IT-intensive banking industry now indicate significant annual labor productivity gains, in contrast to the negative labor productivity changes portrayed under the old method. Producing true output measures for all service industries presents a daunting task. The Bureau of the Census should do more complete surveys of service industries broken down into more detailed and current categories. Even with such data, BEA faces difficult conceptual challenges in developing satisfactory methods for measuring the output of health, legal, business, and other services.

However, BEA has pioneered the use of creative new methods for measuring the quality, price and output changes for computers, semiconductors, and certain telecommunications equipment, along with the development and use of sophisticated methods such as chain-weighted indexes to properly gauge real output changes in a world with some sharply falling prices. Without these statistical advances, it would not have been possible to assess the contribution of IT at the macroeconomic level. In the absence of more accurate measures of output for IT-intensive services industries, we cannot rule out the possibility that IT has made a very modest contribution to labor productivity outside the IT producing sector itself.

Students are assigned to do their research on the Web, at home and not just in the library. Increasingly, job-seekers find job openings on the Web. Sign-up lists passed around at the PTA or other local organizations include a column for e-mail addresses, along with name and telephone number. In each instance, the Internet provides the means for communicating information critical for students, job-seekers, and members of organizations, that could not occur as effectively in other ways. In 1998, 42 percent of all American households had computers at home, and 22 percent had Internet connections at home. Some groups, however, are better networked.

Among the 5.5 million White, Asian, and Pacific Islander families with incomes of at least $75,000, living in a metropolitan area, headed by someone with at least a college education and age 30 to 55, 87 percent had computers at home, and 68 percent had Internet connections. Among households with these levels of income, education, age and living in a metropolitan area, Black and Hispanic households were just as likely to have home computers - but roughly 14 percent less likely to have Internet access at home - as White, Asian, and Pacific Islander households in the same income, education and age group.

Since 1998, more households have obtained computers and Internet access and alternative points of access, such as state employment commission offices, public libraries, and community centers and clubs, have expanded. When the results from a new Census Bureau August survey of households become available this Fall, we will learn the extent to which different groups have improved their access to the Web and capacity to create networks on the Internet.

4

Multicultural Disparities

Despite the rapid increase in computer use and Internet access during the late 1990s, there is still a formidable gap that separates the haves from the have-nots. The term digital divide entered in the mid-1990s in response to the large gap in computer and Internet access separating haves and have-nots. Particularly in the early days, when computers were more expensive and the Web was still the domain of scientists and scholars, it was widely believed that low- and middle-income families would not benefit from these new tools.

Over the years, the costs of having a home computer and an Internet connection have become more affordable to the majority of families in devloped countries, but there are still a large number of low-income families who are left behind. It is important to recognize, however, that access is just the first step in bridging the gap. For example, in US, families with people are more likely than ever to own a computer and be connected to the Internet. All boats are rising, but poor and minority people are playing catch-up to their more affluent, white peers-both at home and in the classroom. Almost all upper-income households have computers, yet only one-third of households with children and a family income of less than $15,000 had a computer in 2001.

Over the past several years, the number of American children with access to information technology has improved. Between 1993 and 2001, the share of all children (ages 3-17) living in households with computers increased from 32 percent to 71 percent. In addition, access to school computers further reduces the number of school-age (5-17) children who have no access to information technology. Data from September 2001 show that about 25 percent of school-age children were able to access computers at school even though they did not have one at home. Nonetheless, 7 percent of teens ages 14 to 17 and 16 percent of kids ages 5 to 9 had no access to computers, either at home or at school. Access to the Internet is still relatively low-less than 60 percent of kids who have a computer at home also use the Internet at home-but home access to the Internet is expanding even more rapidly than computer availability.

Research showing that home access to technology can improve education outcomes for at-risk children makes it even more important that policymakers ensure that these children can take advantage of these powerful tools. As the data below demonstrate, a disproportionate number of the children who have no access to home computers are from low-income and minority families. Much of the disparity in home computer ownership is due to income: Ninety-five percent of children in households earning $75,000 or more a year had a computer at home in 2001, compared to 33 percent of children in households earning $15,000 or less a year. Children from homes with higher incomes also have a rate of home Internet access that is more than 4 times that for poor children.

Internet connections at home are available to almost 63 percent of children living in house-holds in the highest income category, but to only 14 percent of children in the lowest. Furthermore, research documents significant differences in the ways that children from various income groups use their home computers. Compared to their wealthier peers, low-income children are less likely to use their home computers for word processing, school assignments, and other standard software applications and more likely to use them for games.These results confirm that while access is the first barrier to overcome, training in 21st-century literacy skills as well as parental involvement are also necessary.

Geographic fault lines often have been used to characterize the digital divide. For example, in US when introducing the "E-Rate" program in 1998, national leaders pointed out that these new tools made it possible for a child in the most isolated inner-city neighbourhood or rural community to have access to the same world of knowledge at the same instant as a child in the most affluent suburb. While access improved for all children throughout the 1990s, conspicuous inequities and geographic disparities still persist.

Between 1997 and 2001, there were huge increases in the rate of home computer access for black and Hispanic children. The share of black children living in a home with a computer grew from 24 percent in 1997 to 46 percent in 2001, a 92 percent increase. For Hispanic children, home access to a computer more than doubled, from 23 percent in 1997 to 47 percent in 2001. During the same period, the rate for non-Hispanic white children increased by 34 percent. Despite a rapid increase in computer availability for minority children, a large racial gap remains. In 2001, 83 percent of non-Hispanic white children lived in households with computers, compared to only 46 percent of black children and 47 percent of Hispanic children. There are similar gaps in access to the Internet at home. Based on data collected in 2001, 50 percent of non-Hispanic white children were able to connect to the Internet at home, compared to only 25 percent of black children and 20 percent of Hispanic children. While high poverty and lower educational attainment among minority families contribute to their below-average access to home computers and the Internet, they still do not offer a full explanation.

The US Census Bureau data indicate that geography is an important factor affecting children's access. In 2000, only 53 percent of children who lived in central cities had access to a home computer, compared to 61 percent of rural children and 73 percent of children living in suburbs. Similarly, only 24 percent of children in central cities use the Internet at home, compared to 29 percent of rural kids and 35 percent of suburban kids. In its 2001, "A Nation Online," the US Commerce Department acknowledged that during the past few years, Internet access increased more rapidly in rural areas than in central cities. In rural areas, people over the age of 3 who used the Internet from any location jumped from 29 percent in 1998 to 53 percent in 2001. In contrast to this strong growth in rural areas, central-city residents have not kept pace with national-level increases between 1998 and 2001.

The rate of Internet use from any location for people in central cities was only 2 percentage points lower than the national rate in 1998-but by 2001, the divide had grown to 5 points, 49 percent versus 54 percent.States range from a high of 69 percent in New Hampshire to a low of 31 percent in Mississippi. There is a striking pattern of low Internet penetration across the South. The 10 states that have 45 percent or fewer households with children able to access the Internet from home are all in the South or Southwest. By contrast, all six states in the New England region have high rates of Internet access. Other states where more than 55 percent of households with children have home Internet access are more geographically diverse, including Alaska, with the second highest access rate (64 percent), followed by Washington (60 percent). The only other states outside the Northeast that have high Internet penetration are Minnesota and Colorado, each at 58 percent, and Utah at 56 percent.

A 2000 US Census Bureau details on computer and Internet access found that schools help close the technology gap for children who lack computers at home. The net result of the effects schools have in giving computer access across income, racial, and ethnic groups is a levelling of the computer access that children of different groups have compared to what they would have had if home were the only place available for them to use computers. Without school computer access, the gap between high-income children and low-income children is 60 percentage points, but schools reduce that gap by two-thirds to 20 percentage points. Data from the US Department of Education demonstrate that schools have experienced a tremendous increase in Internet access in recent years, growing from only 35 percent of public K-12 schools in 1994 to 98 percent in 2000.

While having Internet access at the school level is important, a better measure than school connectedness is how many instructional classrooms include wired computers. At that level, there has been a striking change from only 3 percent of instructional classrooms having an Internet-equipped computer in 1994, to 77 percent of classrooms having one in 2000. No doubt much of this increase is due to an infusion of federal and local funding throughout the 1990s.

While the federal government's 7 percent contribution to overall education spending is relatively small, its share of ed-tech funding is substantial, accounting for 25 percent to 35 percent of all annual K-12 technology funding, depending on the state. By fiscal year 2001, U.S. Department of Education funding for ed-tech programs had risen to $872 million, compared to the $23 million appropriated in 1993. These resources support an array of services, including purchasing computers and software, training teachers, and revamping curriculums. A change in the nation's telecommunications laws in 1996 also provided new resources for schools.

Universal service provisions, traditionally focused on ensuring nationwide phone service at a reasonable cost, were expanded to include discounts on telecommunications services for schools, libraries, and rural health clinics. Included are discounts on phone service, Internet access, internal networks, and related equipment. Local and long-distance telephone companies contribute funding with fees collected from consumers. In the first 4 years, this "E-Rate" program has provided more than $8 billion in discounts to needy schools.

Technical infrastructure is critical, but basic training is also necessary to remove barriers-such as low levels of literacy and lack of computer experience—that hinder effective use of technology by underserved youth. Teacher training is a critical element of effective classroom technology use and must be supported at all levels as a cornerstone of ed-tech policy. Additionally, the availability of high-quality, appropriate content is an essential ingredient, without might have high-speed pipes with little of value for consumers on the other end. Increasingly, states are trying to ensure that students and teachers are computer literate by mandating such proficiency. This is a sensible strategy to help maximize the benefits from the substantial investments in school technology that have been made over the past decade. In 1999, 35 states had passed technology standards for students, and 26 had introduced technology standards for certification and recertification of teachers.

Despite the clear correlation between state poverty rates and computer and Internet access, some states are bucking the odds with innovative programs. Although Florida has the 10th highest child poverty rate, it is ranked 16th in home Internet penetration, as a result of some innovative statewide technology programs, such as putting computers in community centers and providing extra technology investments to low-performing and low-income schools.

Achieving equitable access to technology, and all of the inherent opportunities that it gives young people, will require the highest level of commitment from decision-makers and the public. To reduce or eliminate the digital divide, develop and adopt a comprehensive national agenda that is fully funded and embraced by government, educators, business leaders, philanthropic organizations, and the public at large. That agenda should be considered as crucial as providing national roads and transportation, Social Security for all citizens, and mandatory childhood immunization.

Web Access Among Racial/ethnic Groups in US

Since the mid-1990s, the World Wide Web has been riding an exponential growth curve. Currently, over 43 million hosts are connected to the Internet worldwide. In terms of individual users, somewhere between 40 to 80 million adults in the United States alone have access to around 320 million unique pages of content, globally distributed on arguably one of the most important communication innovations in history. The Internet is expected to do no less than virtually transform society. Yet even as the Internet races ambitiously toward critical mass, some social scientists are beginning to examine carefully the policy implications of current demographic patterns of Internet access and usage. Key demographic variables like income and education drive the policy questions surrounding the Internet.

In US, almost 70 percent of the schools have at least one computer connected to the Internet, less than 15 percent of classrooms have Internet access. Not surprisingly, access is not distributed randomly, but correlated strongly with income and education. A recent study of Internet use among US college freshman found that nearly 83 percent of all new college students report using the Internet for school work, and almost two-thirds use email to communicate. Yet, closer examination suggests a disturbing disparity in access. While 90.2 percent of private college freshman use the Internet for research, only 77.6 percent of students entering public black colleges report doing so. Similarly, although 80.1 percent of private college freshman use email regularly, only 41.4 percent of students attending black public colleges do. Further, although numerous studies suggest that the gender gap in Internet use appears to be closing over time and that Internet users are increasingly coming from the ranks of those with lower education and income, the perception persists that the gap for race is not decreasing.

In another study Hoffman and Novak examined racial differences in Internet access and use at a single time point and found in 1997 that, overall, whites were significantly more likely than African Americans to have a home computer in their household and also slightly more likely to have PC access at work. Whites were also significantly more likely to have ever used the Web at home, whereas African Americans were slightly more likely to have ever used the Web at school. As one might expect, increasing levels of income corresponded to an increased likelihood of owning a home computer, regardless of race. Although income explained race differences in computer ownership and Web use, education did not. That is, they found that whites were still more likely to own a home computer than were African Americans and to have used the Web recently, despite controlling for differences in education. Their most striking findings, however, were for students. Hoffman and Novak found no differences among white and African American students when students had a home computer. However, among students without a computer in the home, white students were much more likely than African American students to have used the Web, and also more likely to have used the Web at locations other than home, work or school. They concluded that "access translates into usage," and that whites are more likely than African Americans to use the Web because they are more likely to have access.

In 1998, the Commerce Department's National Telecommunications and Information Administration analyzed data on computer penetration rates from the October 1997 Census Current Population Survey (CPS) as part of an ongoing examination of the digital divide. The survey concluded that the gap between the technology "haves" and "have-nots" had increased between 1994 and 1997, with African Americans and Hispanics actually farther behind whites in terms of home computer ownership and Internet access and with an even wider gap between individuals at upper and lower income levels. In an investigation of home computer ownership and Internet use among low-income individuals and minorities in US, Babb, Stephanie F., found that African Americans and Hispanics were less likely to own computers, even after adjusting for income and education and termed this finding, consistent across seven different data sets under examination, "the single most important finding" of her study. Interestingly, some have suggested that United States policy itself may be a contributing factor in the growing digital divide. Cooper and Kimmelman argue that the Telecommunications Act of 1996 has had the unintended and unfortunate consequence of increasing the division between the telecommunications "haves" and "have-nots."

A comparative analysis of web usage and access across racial/ethnic groups in the United States will help us to study the digital disparities in detail. The analysis is based on primary data from three population projectable, US representative surveys of Internet use among Americans, including the first survey on Internet use to collect data on race and ethnicity. The three surveys are Spring 1997 CommerceNet/Nielsen Internet Demographic Study (IDS) conducted in December 1996 and January 1997; Fall 1997 IDS, conducted in August and September 1997; and Spring 1998 IDS, conducted in May and June 1998. Hereafter, these studies will be referred to as the IDS 2, IDS 3, and IDS 4, respectively. The IDS 2, conducted in December 1996/January 1997, was the first nationally projectable survey of Internet usage to collect data on race and ethnicity. That permited us, for the first time, to obtain baseline estimates of differences in Internet and Web use among racial and ethnic groups in the United States. The IDS 3 and IDS 4 also included race and ethnicity, permitting changes to be tracked over time. Additionally, the survey instruments used in IDS 3 and 4 were identical, though slightly modified from IDS 2, thereby ensuring complete comparability across two of the three surveys, and reasonable comparability from IDS 2 to IDS 3 and IDS 4. Each CommerceNet/ Nielsen IDS is based upon an unrestricted random digit dial sampling frame, and used a computer assisted telephone interviewing system to obtain respondents. Eligible respondents were persons 16 years and older in the U.S. and Canada. When weighted, the respondents represent and allow projection to the total population of individuals in the United States aged 16 and over. Respondent weights in the IDS were adjusted by Nielsen so that marginal weighted distributions of Education, Gender, Race, Hispanic Origin, and Age were equivalent to Census estimates for the US and Canada. The particulars of each survey are summarized below.

	Spring 1997 IDS	Fall 1997 IDS	Spring 1998 IDS
Survey	IDS 2	IDS 3	IDS 4
Time Frame	December 1996 -January 1997	August 1997- September 1997	May 1998 June 1998
NO. of US respondents	5,813	7,157	4,042
Total weighted US population aged 16 and over	199.9 million	202.3 million	202.4 million

Table 1 compares the three CommerceNet/Nielsen Internet Demographic Studies, IDS 2, IDS 3, and IDS 4, conducted in December 1996/January 1997, August/September 1997, and May/June 1998, respectively, to March 1995 Census Current Population Survey (CPS) estimates for key demographic variables. The Nielsen IDS samples are representative of the US population.

By comparing the weighted percentages from each Nielsen IDS with corresponding weighted percentages from the Census CPS, it can be find that the distributions reported in Table 1 differ only slightly. One point of departure is race, specifically the percentages for white and other categories in IDS 2 and 3 and "other" in IDS 4. Note that the Census CPS reports more whites, while the Nielsen IDS 2 and 3 report more "other race.".

Table 2 presents the distributions of key demographic variables for each IDS by race and Hispanic origin, compared to the Census CPS and it can be found that:

— Distributions for whites are comparable and consistent over time.

— African-Americans, in the IDS 2, are both slightly overrepresented in the oldest and youngest age categories and in the lowest and highest education categories. There is a larger difference in IDS 2 and 4 for ages 25-45, with African Americans underrepresented in this age group. In the IDS 3, African Americans are overrepresented in the oldest age category and the highest education category, while high school graduates are underrepresented. In IDS 4, African Americans are older and less educated. In IDS 2, 3, and 4, there are more African American students and women than in the Census CPS.

Table 1:
Demographic Comparisons of the Three CommerceNet/Nielsen Internet Demographic Studies with the 1995 Census CPS (US Population Aged 16 and Older)

	CommerceNet/Nielsen Internet Demographic Survey						1995 CPS
	IDS2		IDS3		IDS4		
	Raw	Weighted	Raw	Weighted	Raw	Weighted	Weighted
	Count	%	Count	%	Count	%	%
Age:							
<25	909	15.37	1,024	15.30	608	15.29	16.3
25-45	2,780	43.39	3,295	42.95	1,738	42.32	43.9
46-64	1,402	25.35	1,743	25.90	1,034	26.55	24.0
>64	722	15.89	1,095	15.85	662	15.84	15.7
Total	5,813	100%	7,157	100%	4,042	100%	100%
Education:							
less than h.s.	659	21.89	830	21.88	478	21.88	21.9
high school grad	1,723	31.98	2,007	31.98	1,167	32.01	32.3
some college	1,641	25.44	2,330	25.39	1,303	25.40	25.6
college grad	1,790	20.69	1,990	20.75	1,094	20.71	20.2
Total	5,813	100%	7,157	100%	4,042	100%	100%
Gender:							
Male	2,444	48.01	2,954	48.03	1,624	48.02	48.1
Female	3,369	51.99	4,203	51.97	2,418	51.98	51.9
Total	5,813	100%	7,157	100%	4,042	100%	100%

Student status:							
Full time	469	8.51	523	8.06	296	8.55	7.7
None/part time	5,318	91.49	6,615	91.94	3,726	91.45	92.3
Total	5,787	100%	7,138	100%	4,022	100%	100%
Race:							
White	4,906	78.59	6,000	79.54	3,447	83.41	84.0
African American	493	11.75	691	11.75	441	11.76	11.7
Asian	127	2.09	130	1.99	97	3.03	2.6
American Indian	75	1.62	101	1.85	57	1.80	0.5
Other	212	5.95	235	4.87	0	0	1.2
Total	5,813	100%	7,157	100%	4,042	100%	100%
Ethnicity:							
Hispanic	319	9.51	448	9.50	164	9.51	9.3
Non-Hispanic	5,494	90.49	6,709	90.50	3,878	90.49	90.7
Total	5,813	100%	7,157	100%	4,042	100%	100%.7

Table 2

Demographic Distributions over Time Conditional on Race and Ethnicity of the Three CommerceNet/Nielsen Internet Demographic Studies Compared to the 1995 Census CPS (US Population Aged 16 and Older)

	White				African American				Hispanic			
	IDS2	IDS3	IDS4	CPS	IDS2	IDS3	IDS4	CPS	IDS2	IDS3	IDS4	CPS
N	4,906	6,000	3,447		493	691	441		319	448 1	64	
Age:												
<25	12.79	13.87	13.81	15.5	22.63	19.18	21.16	20.8	31.63	22.02	23.44	23.5
25-45	43.53	41.38	42.03	43.1	38.66	47.20	39.92	47.5	51.04	52.19	43.11	50.6
46-64	26.75	27.72	27.63	24.7	20.81	19.27	24.49	20.7	13.34	17.32	23.08	18.2
>64	16.94	17.03	16.53	16.8	17.84	14.35	14.44	11.0	3.98	8.47	10.36	7.7
Total	*100%*	*100%*	*100%*	*100%*	*100%*	*100%*	*100%*	*100%*	*100%*	*100%*	*100%*	*100%*
Education:												
less thanh.s.	18.56	18.69	19.11	20.4	35.93	31.65	38.18	30.2	36.67	49.47	44.22	48.9
high sc grad	33.45	33.38	32.64	32.5	27.27	27.58	28.66	34.1	24.68	25.47	23.73	25.4
some college	26.44	25.66	26.28	25.8	20.30	26.54	22.86	24.6	26.16	16.69	21.70	18.2
college grad	21.56	22.27	21.97	21.3	16.50	14.23	10.30	11.1	12.49	8.37	10.35	7.5
Total	*100%*	*100%*	*100%*	*100%*	*100%*	*100%*	*100%*	*100%*	*100%*	*100%*	*100%*	*100*
Gender:												
Male	47.87	48.09	49.07	48.5	42.32	43.86	40.41	45.1	46.09	49.09	45.54	50.2
Female	52.13	51.91	50.93	51.5	57.68	56.14	59.59	54.9	53.91	50.91	54.46	49.8
Total	100%	100%	100%	100%	100%	100%	100%	100%	100%	100%	100%	100%\
Studentstatus:												
Full time	6.94	7.45	7.32	7.3	12.98	10.64	11.21	9.4	19.36	8.91	15.48	8.2
None/pttime	93.06	92.55	92.68	92.7	87.02	89.36	88.79	90.6	80.64	91.09	84.52	91.8
Total	*100%*	*100%*	*100%*	*100%*	*100%*	*100%*	*100%*	*100%*	*100%*	*100%*	*100%*	*100%.*

— Results for Hispanics, particularly in the IDS 4, and to a lesser extent in IDS 2, are based upon smaller numbers of respondents and in some cases exhibit substantial departures from Census CPS demographic distributions. IDS 2 Hispanic respondents were much more likely to be younger, more highly educated, and students. In IDS 4, Hispanics were more likely to be older and better educated, female, and full time students. Sample sizes permitting, comparisons of Hispanics with other groups will need to statistically adjust for these demographic variables, before final conclusions can be drawn.

— Due to the large samples sizes for whites and African-Americans, the majority of the analyses contrast whites and African-Americans.

The comparisons in Table 2 are important because they point out the challenges inherent in obtaining truly representative weighted samples. Additionally, these comparisons illustrate that readers must be careful when generalizing survey sample results to determine how the weighted sample compares to the population. Schement presents a detailed discussion of the overlap between Census race categories of white, African-American, Native American, and Asian-American and the ethnic categories of Hispanic/non-Hispanic.

Demographic Differences in Web Across

The major demographic differences between whites and African-Americans occur for age and income. The youngest (16-24) age segment differentiates usage segments more for African-Americans than for whites. African American Web users are more likely to be under 25, across all three surveys.

Overall, Web users are more likely to be under 46 years of age. Web users are more likely to have some college or a college degree, although African American Web users are more likely to have less than high school education than white Web users.

Tables 3a and 3b may provide evidence of an education-driven digital divide. However, it is larger for African Americans than for whites, though it appears to narrow in IDS 4. Of African Americans with no Internet access, 70.27% were high school graduates or had less than a high school education in IDS 2, compared with only 62.11% of whites in the same educational categories with no Internet access.

Of course, African Americans are more likely, in general, to have less education, so this result requires further study. Similarly, of African American Web users, 56.34% had some college or college degrees in IDS 2, compared with 70.89% of white Web users. This gap also does not appear to be diminishing over time. However, to the extent that African Americans are less likely to have some college or a college degree, this result is tentative.

The professional, homemaker, full-time student, and retired/not currently working categories were self-identified single-response. The white-collar category included those respondents who indicated their primary occupation was either technical, administrative/managerial, clerical, sales, or service worker. The blue collar included those respondents who indicated their primary occupation was laborer or craftsman/craftswoman.

Due to its extremely low representation in the sample, respondents indicating they were in the military were excluded from analyses including the occupation variable. For this reason, the Occupation column totals may not necessarily sum to 100 percent. Web users are most likely to be professional, white collar, and students, regardless of race. The percentage of African American Web users who are blue-collar workers has more than tripled over time.

The lowest incomes group (<$40K) differentiate usage segments much more for African-Americans than for whites. Of African-Americans with no Internet access, 80.72% had household incomes less than $40,000 in IDS 2, compared with only 60.9% of whites with no Internet access. Thus, within African-Americans, the income-driven "digital divide" appears larger than for whites. Further, it is not diminishing over time. Again, however, African Americans are more likely to have lower incomes than whites, so these results are tentative until further study. Similarly, of African American Web users, 59.73% had household incomes above $40,000 in IDS 2, compared with 71.01% of white Web users. This gap has also not diminished over time. This concern of an ever-widening gap within African-American income segments has been identified by sociologists as a serious concern.

Katz & Aspden reported evidence of what Lloyd Morrisett of the Markle Foundation has termed a "digital divide", with Internet users being generally wealthier and more highly educated. Sparrow and Vedantham summarize the broader information technology situation as follows: "Information technologies include basic telephone service, personal computing, and computer networking. Although these technologies are becoming everyday conveniences for many Americans, some communities are being left out. Disparities exist in levels of access between rich and poor and between suburban and inner-city residents."

Tables 3a, 3b, and 3c show evidence of a digital divide for both whites and African-Americans.Within both racial groups, "Web users" were most likely to be among the wealthiest individuals, while the "no Internet access segment" was the most likely to be composed of individuals with the lowest incomes. The same holds true for Education. The "Web user" segment was most likely to consist of individuals with some college or who had completed college, while the "no access" segment was most likely to be composed of those with a high school education or less. All these effects were more pronounced for African Americans than whites and these effects appear to persist over time.

There are differences among whites, African Americans and Hispanics in Web use. The statistics on recent Web use for each IDS are presented below.

Aggregate recent web use over time (in millions)

	IDS 2	IDS 3	IDS 4
Raw-count	1555	2305	1562
Recent web-users	45.02	56.23	69.55
% recent web users	22.5	27.8	34.4
Total no.of people	199.93	202.34	202.37

Recent web use over time by bace (in millions)

	White			African			Hispanic		
	IDS2	IDS3	IDS4	IDS2	IDS3	IDS4	IDS2	IDS3	IDS4
Raw-count	1304	2015	1368	104	151	117	91	96	56
Recent web-users	35.22	48.36	60.41	3.9	4.04	5.21	4.79	2.91	5.38
% recent web users	22.4	30.04	35.78	16.6	16.97	21.89	25.2	15.16	28.02
Total no.of people	157.12	160.95	168.81	23.5	23.8	23.8	19.01	19.2	19.2

In IDS 2, 16.6% of African-Americans had used the Web in the six months preceeding the survey. This translated into 3.9 million African-American Web users at the beginning of 1997.

Table 3a:
Demographic Differences Over Time in Web Access and Use for Whites

	IDS2			IDS3			IDS4		
	no-access	*access-only*	*web-user*	*no-access*	*access-only*	*web-user*	*no-access*	*access-only*	*web-user*
N	2,825	569	1,365	3,183	569	2,227	1,630	285	1,522
Age:									
<25	7.41	15.66	25.39	6.81	11.14	26.58	7.10	8.50	23.49
25-45	38.95	50.04	52.74	36.02	46.90	48.75	34.81	46.30	50.57
46-64	29.61	25.52	19.52	29.63	34.15	22.93	29.99	38.09	22.35
>64	24.02	8.78	2.35	27.54	7.81	1.74	28.10	7.11	3.59
Total	*100%*	*100%*	*100%*	*100%*	*100%*	*100%*	*100%*	*100%*	*100%*
Education:									
less than h.s.	21.93	13.38	11.64	21.99	12.33	14.66	25.04	9.62	13.22
high school grad	40.18	30.74	17.46	42.23	35.75	17.69	43.01	37.84	18.60
some college	23.68	30.79	31.58	22.37	30.18	30.13	21.39	38.78	29.77
college grad	14.20	25.09	39.31	13.41	21.74	37.51	10.56	13.76	38.41
Total	*100%*	*100%*	*100%*	*100%*	*100%*	*100%*	*100%*	*100%*	*100%*
Occupation:									
Professional	12.28	22.33	26.33	11.33	17.51	26.24	11.00	17.67	27.64
White collar	28.51	38.76	39.16	27.16	38.27	38.95	23.76	37.82	38.40
Blue collar	13.68	9.64	5.63	15.16	15.14	7.04	16.65	15.96	7.34
Homemaker	13.92	9.32	3.80	13.94	11.16	4.47	16.43	9.38	4.29
Student	2.13	9.59	18.28	1.64	7.46	17.78	1.42	5.78	15.27
Retired	29.10	9.63	4.85	30.77	10.45	5.52	30.40	12.74	5.78
Total	*100%*	*99.26%*	*98.06%*	*100%*	*100%*	*100%*	*99.67%*	*99.36%*	*98.72%*

Household Income									
<$10K	11.49	3.79	2.59	12.80	3.10	2.87	13.60	5.51	2.53
$10K - $19,9	14.12	6.73	5.34	15.87	8.65	5.01	15.91	9.11	4.47
$20K - $29,9	17.67	12.47	9.69	18.97	14.28	9.63	17.39	15.60	10.16
$30K - $39,9	17.62	16.20	11.36	17.35	14.37	13.48	18.31	12.37	11.65
$40K - $59,9	20.93	28.41	27.44	21.14	30.53	26.13	19.21	30.46	25.95
$60K +	18.17	32.39	43.57	13.87	29.07	42.88	15.58	26.95	45.24
Total	*100%*	*100%*	*100%*	*100%*	*100%*	*100%*	*100%*	*100%*	*100%*
Gender:									
Male	43.65	48.22	60.68	44.96	44.51	54.66	44.71	45.37	55.40
Female	56.35	51.78	39.32	55.04	55.49	45.34	55.29	54.63	44.60
Total	*100%*	*100%*	*100%*	*100%*	*100%*	*100%*	*100%*	*100%*	*100%*
% orcolumn who…									
Owns a PC?	26.52	63.43	81.86	23.61	54.51	77.57	21.63	51.28	77.57
PC access at work?	23.39	58.43	68.16	26.32	58.18	64.48	23.75	54.89	63.05

Table 3b:
Demographic Differences Over Time in Web Access and Use for African Americans

	IDS2			IDS3			IDS4		
	no-access	*access-only*	*web-user*	*no-access*	*access-only*	*web-user*	*no-access*	*access-only*	*web-user*
N	298	73	109	387	108	190	266	30	144
Age:									
<25	16.20	21.25	46.30	13.00	17.53	38.51	10.78	5.46	49.47
25-45	37.23	53.43	39.13	46.72	51.82	50.12	38.40	47.24	41.76
46-64	22.76	21.04	14.10	22.02	22.96	11.01	28.68	46.46	8.31
>64	23.80	4.28	0.47	18.27	7.70	0.35	22.15	0.84	0.47
Total	*100%*	*100%*	*100%*	*100%*	*100%*	*100%*	*100%*	*100%*	*100%*
Education:									
less than h.s.	40.52	16.09	29.45	36.57	25.39	16.37	41.57	38.27	30.63
high school grad	29.75	33.70	14.21	35.35	24.71	11.57	33.00	32.20	17.14
some college	17.71	27.45	26.04	20.70	36.96	37.51	18.75	22.90	32.50
college grad	12.03	25.58	30.30	7.37	12.94	34.54	6.67	6.63	19.74
Total	*100%*	*100%*	*100%*	*100%*	*100%*	*100%*	*100%*	*100%*	*100%*
Occupation:									
Professional	11.32	24.02	28.59	12.36	25.23	26.55	11.84	15.60	18.95
White collar	23.13	35.66	28.56	25.80	39.60	38.91	22.89	54.82	28.94
Blue collar	14.00	7.46	2.99	18.47	10.36	3.08	13.09	18.61	9.61
Homemaker	10.28	2.72	0.00	11.13	3.37	1.10	20.75	0.00	2.15
Student	7.10	17.33	30.46	5.39	9.01	28.36	4.42	3.18	29.60
Retired	33.56	9.87	8.09	26.85	12.43	1.99	25.68	5.29	4.66
Total	*99.39%*	*97.06%*	*98.70%*	*100%*	*100%*	*100%*	*98.67%*	*97.49%*	*93.91%*

Household Income									
<$10K	34.28	9.02	15.62	30.92	12.63	4.55	26.80	4.75	8.56
$10K - $19,9	19.87	11.31	2.90	28.80	12.23	4.24	21.50	22.54	6.98
$20K - $29,9	17.70	22.00	10.63	15.43	19.71	11.93	19.07	27.86	12.44
$30K - $39,9	8.87	8.32	11.23	6.00	16.33	19.36	12.00	14.33	14.48
$40K - $59,9	10.94	24.28	27.43	12.52	26.46	18.81	11.25	19.81	24.75
$60K +	8.34	25.07	32.30	6.33	12.64	41.11	9.38	10.71	32.79
Total	*100%*	*100%*	*100%*	*100%*	*100%*	*100%*	*100%*	*100%*	*100%*
Gender:									
Male	38.15	53.55	55.40	38.68	44.01	55.78	34.10	46.46	53.61
Female	61.85	44.65	44.60	61.32	55.99	44.22	65.90	53.54	46.39
Total	*100%*	*100%*	*100%*	*100%*	*100%*	*100%*	*100%*	*100%*	*100%*
% or column who...									
Owns a PC	16.70	44.18	65.05	14.82	34.53	65.62	12.09	29.30	68.24
PC-access at work	18.74	65.39	63.54	24.49	58.20	67.49	24.45	44.85	63.00.

Table 3c:
Demographic Differences Over Time in Web Access and Use for Hispanics

	IDS2			IDS3			IDS4		
	no-access	*access-only*	*web-user*	*no-access*	*access-only*	*web-user*	*no-access*	*access-only*	*web-user*
N	182	32	93	278	41	121	84	15	61
Age:									
<25	16.85	46.51	55.20	13.92	34.30	47.99	10.01	33.56	46.91
25-45	61.51	36.09	36.39	53.83	58.02	40.92	45.86	41.13	41.22
46-64	16.98	17.40	5.45	21.29	7.68	10.17	30.41	25.32	8.36
>64	4.67	0.00	2.96	10.96	0.00	0.92	13.72	0.00	3.51
Total	*100%*	*100%*	*100%*	*100%*	*100%*	*100%*	*100%*	*100%*	*100%*
Education:									
less than h.s.	35.00	29.67	41.20	55.55	36.21	28.85	52.01	14.60	34.38
high school grad	32.75	28.18	8.64	27.95	35.94	14.11	24.58	37.44	20.62
some college	22.58	29.98	30.62	12.12	21.39	32.49	18.26	43.94	22.37
college grad	9.67	25.78	19.55	4.37	6.46	24.55	5.15	4.02	22.63
Total	*100%*	*100%*	*100%*	*100%*	*100%*	*100%*	*100%*	*100%*	*100%*
Occupation:									
Professional	11.83	14.18	16.22	6.95	11.22	21.77	8.93	16.14	23.32
White collar	28.59	32.88	30.62	26.86	30.59	43.83	16.35	45.55	30.77
Blue collar	19.37	8.35	4.36	25.62	35.24	4.91	14.02	0.00	0.00
Homemaker	19.52	3.62	2.07	20.09	0.00	0.62	37.98	0.00	2.52
Student	5.60	40.97	38.14	3.75	17.51	26.32	3.20	33.56	35.50
Retired	14.50	0.00	7.37	16.73	5.44	2.54	18.05	4.76	2.37
Total	*99.42%*	*100%*	*98.77%*	*100%*	*100%*	*100%*	*98.53%*	*100%*	*94.48%*

Household Income									
<$10K	10.33	3.70	12.24	20.94	29.03	5.85	20.25	4.01	10.79
$10K - $19,9	30.70	2.54	13.11	32.70	16.75	3.50	27.38	0.00	6.10
$20K - $29,9	19.09	4.50	11.65	21.78	17.12	9.39	19.79	20.13	7.23
$30K - $39,9	14.34	27.27	10.29	11.20	10.67	16.03	10.34	9.06	8.05
$40K - $59,9	15.02	25.24	18.83	9.25	21.84	24.56	10.22	12.69	25.81
$60K + 10.52	36.77	33.87	4.14	4.59	40.67	12.02	54.11	42.02	
Total	*100%*	*100%*	*100%*	*100%*	*100%*	*100%*	*100%*	*100%*	*100%*
Gender:									
Male	42.93	38.91	56.35	45.42	63.21	55.60	31.99	40.72	70.86
Female	57.07	61.09	43.65	54.58	36.79	44.40	68.01	59.28	29.14
Total	*100%*	*100%*	*100%*	*100%*	*100%*	*100%*	*100%*	*100%*	*100%*
% or column who...									
Owns a PC	26.26	58.21	61.99	13.90	36.16	72.00	11.54	20.09	77.45
PC-accessatwork	24.23	50.92	49.58	21.85	61.62	59.52	19.02	54.52	50.00

Race Differences Over Time in Web Use

A series of comparisons among whites, African-Americans and Hispanics on key indicators of Web access and use are presented in Table 4. In IDS 2, overall, whites were more likely than African-Americans to have access to the Internet, and to have ever used the Web. Whites were also more likely to own a computer, have PC access at work, and have fax, cable, and a satellite dish at home. The percentages of access and use for both whites and African Americans has increased over time, but the gaps persist. In fact, the overall gap between whites and African Americans in Internet access and having ever used have actually increased over time.

In IDS 2, 35.8% of whites had Internet access, compared to 31.68% of African Americans. By IDS 4, although 49.33% of whites had access, the percentage of African Americans with Internet access had risen only a few percentage points, to 35.54%. Similarly, in IDS 2, 24.34% of whites had ever used the Internet, compared to 18.76% of African Americans. In IDS 4, eighteen months later 40.37% of whites had ever used the Internet, compared to 27.98% of African Americans. Although whites are still more likely to own a PC and to have PC access at work, these gaps have not increased over time. Further, the gaps in cable and satellite ownership have disappeared. In fact, satellite penetration has doubled among African Americans and the penetration rate in IDS 4 equals that for whites. The gap between whites and African-Americans in computer ownership has been cited as the key explanation for corresponding gaps in Web usage. A Yankelovich Monitor study "suggests that what bars entry to cyberspace among African Americans is owning a home PC, not lack of interest in the Internet."

However, a Forrester Research study cites "technology optimism" as an important predictor of technology adoption. Further research is required to understand these increasing gaps in access and usage. A number of reasons have been provided in the popular press for the gap between whites and African-Americans in computer ownership. Price and value are often cited as explanations.

The PC penetration rates are not increasing overall among African Americans. Although the percentage of whites owning a home computer has increased slightly over time, approaching fifty percent, the overall percentage of African Americans who own a home computer has remained at 29%. Overall, the gap in access and use is persistent and appears to be increasing. In IDS 2, whites were more frequent and more recent Web users than African Americans. White recent Web users in IDS 2 were also more likely to have ever used the Web from home and work, while recent African American Web users were more likely to have ever used the Web from school. African Americans in IDS 2 were much more likely to be newer users, and whites were much more likely to have been using the Web for two years or more. But over time, is apparent that African American Web users have made significant gains in Web use. Indeed, the gaps are diminishing rapidly.

The gap in Web use at home has decreased dramatically and African Americans now appear to be more likely than whites to have ever used the Web from work, school or other locations. Additionally, African American Web users are becoming more recent and more frequent Web users. In fact, differences between white and African American Web users in their recency and frequency of Web use have disappeared. African

Table 4: Race and ethnicity differences over time on key web usage variables

	White			African American			Hispanic		
	IDS2	IDS3	IDS4	IDS2	IDS3	IDS4	IDS2	IDS3	IDS4
Among all respondents									
N	4,906	6,000	3,447	493	691	441	319	448	164
Current Access	35.84	43.25	49.33	31.68	38.99	35.54	38.64	29.84	39.73
Ever used	24.34	33.56	40.37	18.76	23.22	27.98	28.06	19.73	31.77
Own a PC	44.24	44.62	46.66	28.92	29.05	29.07	39.86	26.86	32.33
PC access at work	38.23	42.07	42.35	32.97	38.96	36.70	33.56	32.31	31.52
Home fax	14.00	13.68	14.86	9.04	7.26	8.03	14.31	8.72	14.29
Cable	68.46	72.87	74.49	63.36	72.87	75.11	65.61	63.87	68.30
Satellite	10.55	11.96	13.52	5.06	7.49	12.69	7.74	7.27	11.23
Among Recent Web Users									
N	1,304	2,015	1,368	104	151	117	91	96	56
First Used									
...in past 2 years +	16.17	33.14	49.47	6.79	31.91	43.98	14.96	27.28	48.94
...in past 1-2 years	18.41	23.95	19.99	15.78	20.77	17.61	5.01	22.86	16.94
...in past year	22.40	23.77	15.69	15.42	26.09	19.46	22.10	31.27	18.13
...in past 6 months	18.65	9.39	8.81	18.39	9.23	6.10	21.35	11.88	5.59
...in past 3 months	24.36	9.74	6.05	43.62	12.00	12.85	36.58	6.71	10.10
Last Used									
...in past 6 months	8.40	7.68	5.37	10.50	4.70	2.32	8.70	4.67	6.58
...in past 3 months	12.09	11.67	6.57	30.94	21.19	11.46	10.18	15.35	0.56
...in past month	21.95	19.38	19.30	23.77	26.86	21.44	33.68	23.34	23.92
...in past week	27.89	26.81	30.19	18.90	25.62	35.62	32.18	23.62	39.01
...in past 24 hours	29.68	34.46	38.56	15.88	21.63	29.17	15.25	33.02	29.94

Frequency of Use									
...once a day +	18.49	22.20	26.79	15.33	15.67	25.33	10.31	25.94	30.97
...few times/week	28.59	29.30	31.54	25.92	27.97	32.26	36.44	29.34	31.30
...two-four times/month	26.67	24.77	25.03	28.25	26.10	23.28	28.05	30.76	30.42
...once a month or less	26.25	23.73	16.64	30.50	30.26	19.13	25.21	19.96	7.31
Ever Used									
...at home	61.36	64.94	68.85	46.44	55.02	60.83	35.98	65.74	73.34
...at work	44.15	51.77	50.55	36.73	63.37	61.06	32.07	44.83	44.69
...at school	28.31	29.26	28.79	44.39	40.18	57.07	48.58	32.58	51.84
...at other locations	26.22	39.40	35.06	24.39	48.36	53.69	30.28	50.29	46.87.2

Americans are still among the newest users, but are now also joining the ranks of the long-term users. By IDS 4, 43.98 percent of African American recent Web users, compared to 49.47 percent of white recent Web users, had been using the Web for two years or more.

Student Status

The differences on most indicators of Internet access and use, and also home computer ownership between whites and African-Americans is greater for student than non-students White non-students in IDS 2 were more likely to have access to the Web, to have ever used the Web, to own a PC, and have PC access at work. Additionally, white non-students were also more likely than African Americans to have a home fax, cable, and a satellite dish. Over time, and similar to the previous analysis, overall differences between white and African American non-students actually appear to be increasing. Note that the percentage of white non-students who own a home computer is increasing slightly, but that the percentage of African American non-students who own a home computer is actually decreasing over time. At the same time, the percentages of African American non-students who have cable or a satellite dish have increased and are now similar to the penetration rates for whites.

Since IDS 2, African Americans are increasingly likely to have been using the Web for two years or more, more likely to have ever used the Web at home, work, school, or other locations, and more likely to be more recent and frequent users of the Web. However, white non-student recent Web users are making similar gains, and in some cases, their use still outpaces that of African Americans. For example, whites are still more likely to be among the most recent Web users. In IDS 4, 39.96 percent of whites reported using the Web in the past 24 hours, compared to 30.55 percent of African Americans. On the other hand, differences in Web use frequency between white and African American non-student recent Web users have disappeared. Additionally, African American non-students are more likely to have used the Web from work, school or other locations.

African American non-students are significantly less likely to own a home computer than white non-students (and in fact, even less likely over time), and consequently exhibit lower overall rates of access and usage. Yet, among recent Web users, who by definition have access somewhere, recency and frequency usage rates for African American respondents has over time come to mirror that of whites.

Table 5b shows clearly that, overall, Web access, usage and PC penetration rates are considerably higher for students than non-students, regardless of race. Additionally, Web access, usage and PC penetration rates are all rising over time, for both white and African American students. In fact, 53.83 percent of African American students owned a home computer in IDS 4, compared with only 25.67 percent of African American non-students. Eighteen months earlier, in IDS 2, the PC penetration rate was considerably lower: only 31.88 percent of African American students, compared with 28.66 percent of African American non-students, owned a home PC. At the same time, Table 5b reveals clear disparities in Internet access and use between African American and white students. For example, though both groups have higher rates over time, white students are more likely to have Web access, and to have ever used the Web, and these differences persist over time.

White students are more likely to own home computers than African American students and this difference remains over time, despite the fact that home computer ownership over time among white students is flat and home computer ownership among African American students has been steadily and impressively rising. However, the gaps in access and usage are clearly decreasing over time and this may in part be due to increasing rates of PC ownership among African American students. Additionally, African American students were more likely to have access to a PC at work in IDS 4. Thus, one could hypothesize that as PC ownership and PC access rates continue to rise, so will overall Web access and usage rates. African American recent Web user students, like their white counterparts, are increasingly likely to be more recent and more frequent Web users. In fact, the differences between the two groups, as for non-students, have effectively disappeared. However, white students are still more likely to have ever used the Web from home, while African American students are more likely to have ever used the Web from work and school.

Home Computer Ownership

Table 6a compares Web access and usage patterns for white and African American non-students who do not own a home computer. Table 6b shows the same comparison for white and African American non-students who do own a home computer. The presence of a computer in the home has a dramatic impact overall on access and usage. Non-student respondents, regardless of race, are much more likely to have access to the Web and to have ever used the Web if they own a home computer.

Table 5a: *Race and ethnicity differences over time on key web usage variables for non-students*

	White			African American			Hispanic		
	IDS2	IDS3	IDS4	IDS2	IDS3	IDS4	IDS2	IDS3	IDS4
Among all non-student respondents									
N	4,554	5,581	3,212	423	619	388	264	405	138
Current access	32.59	39.60	46.05	27.31	35.29	30.34	29.05	25.59	30.65
Ever used	20.94	29.94	36.89	14.69	18.66	21.98	20.92	15.79	24.17
Own a PC	42.09	42.51	44.90	28.66	27.94	25.67	35.28	24.19	26.32
PC access at work	39.12	43.19	43.06	34.71	40.17	35.61	37.34	32.84	31.18
Home fax	13.70	13.28	14.40	9.27	7.78	8.20	13.25	8.81	13.04
Cable	68.29	72.54	74.49	64.23	73.06	74.91	66.27	64.85	68.92
Satellite	10.69	11.87	13.77	5.02	7.60	11.37	8.39	6.39	9.82
Among recent non-student web users									
N	1,089	1,722	1,194	83	123	88	63	81	41
First Used									
...in past 2 years +	16.74	32.90	49.54	6.99	29.15	37.85	22.65	30.20	56.23
...in past 1-2 years	19.02	22.59	19.37	20.91	20.38	19.96	6.19	20.13	4.41
...in past year	22.62	24.74	15.17	16.70	26.89	20.40	20.85	32.25	18.90
...in past 6 months	18.32	9.50	9.27	19.96	10.19	7.51	16.76	12.96	8.71
...in past 3 months	23.41	10.27	6.65	35.44	13.40	14.28	33.56	4.45	11.75
Last Used									
...in past 6 months	7.65	6.65	5.59	11.54	5.97	3.34	9.38	5.96	7.93
...in past 3 months	12.08	11.07	7.02	31.74	16.26	11.66	5.65	14.04	0.84

...in past month	21.82	19.07	18.81	21.42	28.65	19.48	30.43	21.10	24.93
...in past week	27.28	27.54	28.62	18.26	26.42	34.97	34.72	19.47	32.68
...in past 24 hours	31.17	35.68	39.96	17.04	22.70	30.55	19.82	39.43	33.92
Frequency of Use									
...once a day +	20.08	22.69	28.16	12.61	14.83	24.39	11.37	30.97	39.97
...few times/week	27.54	30.50	31.03	26.28	28.59	34.28	41.27	26.18	30.85
...two-four times/month	26.34	23.72	22.76	25.82	25.61	20.58	26.47	27.33	18.31
...once a month or less	25.73	23.09	18.05	35.59	30.97	20.75	20.88	15.53	10.88
Ever Used									
...at home	63.17	65.54	68.12	49.56	59.94	64.48	41.24	72.63	76.35
...at work	50.74	56.99	55.60	46.64	68.81	66.86	46.92	52.24	59.38
...at school	18.23	19.69	20.77	30.82	29.12	38.67	31.39	29.04	36.01
...at other locations	24.83	36.44	32.59	29.29	42.69	52.35	26.07	44.39	40.62.

Table 5b: Race and ethnicity differences over time on key web usage variables for students

	White			African American			Hispanic		
	IDS2	IDS3	IDS4	IDS2	IDS3	IDS4	IDS2	IDS3	IDS4
Among all student respondents									
N	336	405	218	64	68	50	55	41	26
Current Access	80.33	87.82	90.25	62.78	71.12	74.97	81.87	72.79	87.85
Ever used	62.72	78.15	83.26	43.20	58.16	72.82	55.38	54.66	71.03
Own a PC	72.98	69.24	69.50	31.88	39.77	53.83	58.86	55.16	65.12
PC access at work	26.62	27.97	32.95	22.04	30.67	47.60	17.58	27.98	33.40
Home fax	18.42	18.19	20.59	7.77	3.09	7.21	18.72	8.27	21.01
Cable	71.54	76.16	74.84	62.21	72.51	75.73	62.88	57.13	64.95
Satellite	9.17	13.50	10.60	4.85	6.95	23.93	5.00	16.66	18.90
Among recent student web users									
N	212	289	170	20	28	29	28	14	15
First Used									
...in past 2 years +	13.81	34.02	48.58	6.29	42.09	57.83	2.02		
...in past 1-2 years	15.85	31.20	23.31	0.00	22.21	12.32	3.03		
...in past year	21.04	19.23	18.66	11.73	23.14	17.35	24.20		
...in past 6 months	20.36	9.02	6.41	13.86	5.70	2.89	29.08		
...in past 3 months	28.94	6.53	2.84	68.12	6.86	9.62	41.68		
Last Used									
...in past 6 months	11.90	12.91	4.28	7.46	0.00	0.00	7.56		
...in past 3 months	11.80	14.87	4.23	29.10	39.42	0.00	17.82		
...in past month	22.09	20.34	22.37	31.66	20.23	5.34	39.16		

...in past week	30.91	22.89	38.63	19.19	22.67	73.28	27.90
...in past 24 hours	23.30	29.00	30.49	12.58	17.67	21.37	7.56
Frequency of Use							
...once a day +	11.60	20.22	18.80	24.09	18.72	27.47	8.52
...few times/week	32.27	23.00	34.32	25.37	25.70	27.66	28.29
...two-four times/month	27.55	29.69	37.66	37.31	27.91	29.42	30.70
...once a month or less	28.58	27.09	9.22	13.22	27.67	15.46	32.49
Ever Used							
...at home	52.80	62.24	70.42	37.63	36.86	52.55	27.11
...at work	15.01	26.65	23.81	6.40	43.26	48.02	7.06
...at school	73.50	76.75	73.69	80.47	98.93	94.79	77.54
...at other locations	32.35	53.92	49.37	9.49	70.35	56.76	37.37

Additionally, among non-students with a home computer, whites are more likely to have access and to have ever used, but the differences are small. Yet, there are striking gaps in access and usage among non-students without a home computer. In IDS 4, whites were more likely than African Americans to have access to and have ever used the Web. Gap in use among non-students without a home computer is increasing over time.

Whites and African Americans have similar rates of usage frequency and recency, suggesting once again, that given access, usage follows for both groups. African Americans without a home computer are more likely than whites to have ever used the Web at school or other locations. Among non-students recent Web users with a home computer, both recency and frequency of Web use increase over time for both whites and African Americans, and differences are diminishing rapidly. By IDS 4, 73.85 percent of white non-students with a home computer had last used the Web within the past week, compared to 67.58% of African Americans and 64.62% of whites had used the Web a few times a week or more, compared to 59.05% of African Americans. Both groups enjoy similarly high percentages of having ever used the Web at home; 80.55% of whites and 82.12% of African Americans in IDS 4 had ever used the Web at home. In IDS 4, African American non-students were more likely than their white counterparts to have ever used the Web at work, at school and at other locations. Tables 6c and 6d show the analysis for students with and without a computer in the home. Sample sizes are much smaller for African-American students when segmented by whether they have a computer at home, so the results must be interpreted with caution.

Compared to Tables 6a and 6b, Tables 6c and 6d show that students are more likely to have access to the Web and to use the Web, compared to non-students. Regardless of race, non-students with a home computer have access and usage rates that are similar to students without a home computer. Students with a home computer enjoy the highest levels of access and use, while non-students without a home computer have the lowest levels of access and use.

Additionally, having a computer in the home leads to much higher levels of Web access and use for students of both races, but the difference is clearly more dramatic for non-students than students.

The differences in access and usage for non-students with and without a home computer are larger than the differences for students with and without a home computer. Presumably this is because students have more opportunities for access at school, even if they do not own a computer at home. However, without a computer in the home, there is a much larger gap between African-American and white students in terms of Web access, and the corresponding percentages of having ever used the Web are also smaller.

In fact, the gap in access for students without a computer in the home appears to be increasing. The presence of a computer in the home is bringing African American and White students to parity in Internet access and Web use. Increasing the Internet access opportunities for students, especially African-American students without home computers, may help to reduce the gaps in access and usage.

Table 6a: Race and ethnicity differences in web access and use by student status and home computer ownership

Non-student respondents without a home computer

	White			African American			Hispanic		
	IDS2	IDS3	IDS4	IDS2	IDS3	IDS4	IDS2	IDS3	IDS4
Among all non-student respondents without a home computer									
N	3,258	3,134	1,733	282	421	271	158	274	94
Current access	13.91	19.35	22.87	14.23	22.77	16.91	17.65	14.39	14.35
Ever used	6.47	11.37	14.84	4.99	7.04	8.84	12.21	5.37	6.29
Among recent non-student web users without a home computer									
N	207	417	276	22	32	24	18	22	12
First Used									
...in past 2 years +	11.45	23.22	37.30	5.98	21.47	34.17			
...in past 1-2 years	8.53	19.76	21.35	8.26	13.04	12.30			
...in past year	21.02	28.09	22.81	21.37	32.34	15.02			
...in past 6 months	22.88	12.57	10.97	35.61	16.71	10.12			
...in past 3 months	36.13	16.36	7.57	28.77	16.44	28.40			
Last Used									
...in past 6 months	17.04	12.64	11.97	31.20	17.53	0.00			
...in past 3 months	15.75	20.00	12.36	25.36	14.95	9.83			
...in past month	30.26	25.54	26.27	12.96	26.36	30.44			
...in past week	21.96	24.35	27.40	22.08	30.43	30.97			
...in past 24 hours	14.99	17.46	22.01	8.40	10.73	27.75			
Frequency of Use									

...once a day +	16.34	13.73	14.13	15.29	7.74	19.77
...few times/week	18.56	20.21	25.20	44.08	38.12	37.84
...two-four times/month	24.22	23.14	28.14	7.65	13.22	22.83
...once a month or less	40.89	42.92	32.53	32.98	40.93	19.56
Ever Used						
...at home	7.54	19.63	24.80	10.83	12.36	14.59
...at work	58.22	56.10	64.99	41.88	69.29	64.27
...at school	21.56	21.11	22.17	35.75	26.52	53.38
...at other locations	33.18	50.40	45.89	31.05	53.94	60.47

Table 6b: Race and ethnicity differences in web access and use by student status and home computer ownership

Non-student respondents with a home computer

	White			African American			Hispanic		
	IDS2	IDS3	IDS4	IDS2	IDS3	IDS4	IDS2	IDS3	IDS4
Among all non-student respondents with a home computer									
N	2,025	2,442	1,479	140	197	116	105	130	44
Current access	58.36	66.87	74.31	59.76	66.56	69.35	50.80	59.76	74.42
Ever used	40.87	55.09	63.82	38.50	48.53	60.19	37.21 48.56	72.72	
Among recent non-student web users with a home computer									
N	882	1,304	918	61	91	64	45	59	29
First Used									
...in past 2 years +	17.88	35.75	52.88	7.31	31.46	39.12	34.10	35.27	59.33
...in past 1-2 years	21.29	23.43	18.83	24.87	22.59	22.59	6.23	22.44	5.85
...in past year	22.84	23.77	13.09	15.24	25.25	22.25	15.50	30.23	13.11
...in past 6 months	17.34	8.55	8.80	15.06	8.22	6.62	10.39	7.32	11.56
...in past 3 months	20.66	8.50	6.40	37.52	12.48	9.42	33.78	4.74	10.15
Last Used									
...in past 6 months	5.61	4.90	3.83	5.39	2.50	4.53	3.82	0.85	1.53
...in past 3 months	11.29	8.41	5.55	33.73	16.35	12.30	6.13	5.97	10.52
...in past month	19.98	17.19	16.76	24.06	29.34	15.59	16.33	37.13	19.04
...in past week	28.44	28.48	28.95	17.07	25.20	36.39	29.15	28.50	19.39
...in past 24 hours	34.68	41.01	44.90	19.74	26.31	31.19	44.57	27.54	49.53

Frequency of Use									
...once a day +	20.88	25.26	32.00	11.81	16.90	26.03	7.73	36.34	51.30
...few times/week	29.83	33.47	32.62	20.99	25.82	33.02	45.92	28.28	28.48
...two-four times/month	26.80	23.84	21.30	30.84	29.21	19.78	28.24	39.47	13.93
...once a month or less	22.49	17.43	14.08	36.36	28.07	21.17	18.11	5.91	6.30
Ever Used									
...at home	75.27	78.97	80.55	61.68	74.26	82.12	57.96	86.96	87.11
...at work	49.12	57.29	53.01	48.13	68.66	67.79	53.76	43.77	44.33
...at school	17.51	19.29	20.39	29.28	29.90	33.47	23.65	33.67	32.93
...at other locations	23.02	32.31	28.94	28.74	39.26	49.48	27.22	43.18	35.85

Table 6c: Race and ethnicity differences in web access and use by student status and home computer ownership

Students without a home computer

	White			African American			Hispanic		
	IDS2	IDS3	IDS4	IDS2	IDS3	IDS4	IDS2	IDS3	IDS4
Among all student respondents without a home computer									
N	89	125	59	42	41	24	22	17	9
Current access	65.14	73.13	78.76	59.65	60.22	61.90	82.49		
Ever used	45.21	65.99	65.78	38.47	51.98	60.02	51.93		

Table 6d: Race and ethnicity differences in web access and use by student status and home computer ownership

Students with a home computer

	White			African American			Hispanic		
	IDS2	IDS3	IDS4	IDS2	IDS3	IDS4	IDS2	IDS3	IDS4
Among all student respondents with a home computer									
N	247	280	159	22	27	26	33	23	17
Current access	85.59	94.40	95.30	69.06	87.61	86.19	81.49	87.63	
Ever used	69.19	83.55	90.93	53.13	67.53	83.80	57.79	64.73	

Education

Tables 7a-7d show the influence of education on Web access and usage between whites and African Americans. In general, increasing levels of education lead to higher levels of Web access, usage, PC ownership and PC access at work. However, these levels are higher for whites than for African Americans and these race differences persist even after adjusting for education. In fact, the gaps in access and usage are largest for those with a college degree.

At the lowest levels of education, whites are more likely than African Americans to have access to the Web, to have ever used the Web, and to own a computer. What is more, these differences persist over time. Among those with less than a high school education, African Americans are gaining ground faster than whites in Web access, use and PC ownership over time. Overall, the gaps are smaller here. Whites are more likely to have access to a PC at work, in IDS 2 and IDS 3. By IDS 4, there is no difference between whites and African Americans with less than a high school education on this variable. However, students are included in this group and that could account for some of these gains.

Among high school graduates, levels of computer ownership among both groups are stagnant, and whites are more likely than African Americans to own a PC. African American high school graduates are more likely to have access to a PC at work than are white high school graduates. Additionally, the gap in access and use between whites and African Americans is larger for high school graduates than for those without a high school degree.

The results for respondents with some college are shown in Table 7c.In IDS 4, whites were more likely to have Web access, to have ever used the Web, and to own a home computer. Except for access, the gaps are diminishing over time. African Americans are more likely to have PC access at work. Larger sample sizes permitted us to examine Web usage patterns among recent Web users with some college. In IDS 2, twice as many African Americans as whites with some college education reported using the Web for the first time (50.62 percent of African Americans compared to 25.25 percent of whites). More than twice as many whites as African Americans reported using the Web for two years or more. Thus, in IDS 2, whites were more likely to be long-term users and African Americans were more likely to be newer users. By IDS 4, similar percentages of African Americans and whites have been using the Web for two years or more; 43.81 percent of whites and 46.59 percent of African Americans had been using the Web for two years or more. In IDS 2, whites were more both recent and frequent users of the Web, compared to African Americans.

Over time, however, these differences have effectively vanished, with 65.82 percent of whites and 66.87 percent of African Americans in IDS 4 reporting using the Web within the past week. Similarly, 29.13 percent of whites and 26.30 percent of African Americans with some college used the Web once a day or more in IDS 4, and African Americans with some college are actually more likely than whites to have used the Web a few times a week. In IDS 2, whites with some college were more likely to have ever used the Web at home and work, and African Americans were more likely to have ever used the Web at school.

Table 7a: Race and ethnicity differences over time on key web usage variables for respondents with less than high school cducation

	White			African American			Hispanic		
	IDS2	IDS3	IDS4	IDS2	IDS3	IDS4	IDS2	IDS3	IDS4
Among all respondents with less than high school education									
N	492	609	360	93	125	98	73	130	41
Current access	23.46	32.89	32.83	21.41	25.92	29.96	40.55	19.35	27.83
Ever used	14.93	26.45	28.26	15.46	11.85	22.40	31.30	11.28	25.15
Own a PC	28.92	31.99	32.60	15.26	10.25	20.70	29.75	15.71	20.39
PC access at work	11.26	16.72	13.28	7.64	10.09	13.73	11.98	16.11	7.83
Home fax	8.29	9.48	9.55	2.40	0.97	6.93	9.60	4.90	7.35
Cable	61.41	69.63	68.88	42.19	62.78	64.48	62.51	54.41	58.62
Satellite	10.82	13.76	13.17	3.89	8.32	16.56	7.33	9.16	13.13

Table 7b: Race and ethnicity differences over time on key web usage variables for respondents with less than high school education

	White			African American			Hispanic		
	IDS2	IDS3	IDS4	IDS2	IDS3	IDS4	IDS2	IDS3	IDS4
Among all high school graduate respondents									
N	1,475	1,710	998	149	187	129	75	122	44
Current access	23.09	28.13	33.35	25.64	23.38	25.37	21.17	24.67	39.15
Ever used	12.42	17.77	22.87	9.39	9.52	16.69	9.46	10.60	26.91
Own a computer	32.31	31.18	35.30	20.26	22.23	21.34	27.33	20.66	32.71
PC access at work	30.01	32.20	31.67	26.98	35.18	36.20	32.21	39.44	34.55
Home fax	8.95	8.69	9.87	7.87	4.30	5.66	6.86	7.59	12.02
Cable	68.61	72.37	74.08	70.69	70.86	81.44	59.29	68.13	68.03
Satellite	12.34	13.72	15.20	3.09	8.20	9.34	9.34	4.98	10.62

Table 7c: Race and ethnicity differences over time on key web usage variables for respondents with some college

Students with a home computer

	White			African American			Hispanic		
	IDS2	IDS3	IDS4	IDS2	IDS3	IDS4	IDS2	IDS3	IDS4
Among All Respondents with Some College									
N	1,397	1,943	1,117	131	242	151	103	127	55
Currently	42.51	50.67	58.85	41.46	53.51	47.25	45.85	50.19	49.06
Have access									
Ever used	28.40	39.40	45.49	23.31	32.06	39.69	31.84	37.23	31.92
Own a computer	53.44	52.03	51.33	44.34	36.37	46.31	52.07	49.03	38.34
PC access at work	47.09	52.98	53.26	49.36	58.22	60.64	47.41	54.14	55.75
Home fax	16.65	15.79	16.60	10.62	10.19	9.99	17.01	12.09	17.98
Cable	70.09	73.24	77.22	75.10	80.42	80.03	69.84	76.92	82.21
Satellite	11.42	12.40	13.51	4.68	7.76	12.60	5.97	6.01	6.11
Among recent web users with some college									
N	388	700	451	32	53	48	29	37	18
First Used									
...in past 2 years +	14.23	31.18	43.81	5.97	20.58	46.59	15.48	12.75	
...in past 1-2 years	19.53	22.24	22.05	1.16	26.86	25.44	8.10	19.07	
...in past year	21.70	26.78	17.08	22.10	29.96	16.62	18.25	46.81	
...in past 6 months	19.28	10.90	9.53	20.14	10.90	3.55	24.04	13.37	
...in past 3 months	25.25	8.89	7.53	50.62	11.70	7.79	34.12	6.01	

Last Used								
...in past 6 months	10.59	6.79	4.89	4.19	5.78	0.00	9.49	7.05
...in past 3 months	12.97	12.04	9.65	27.72	22.24	9.14	13.97	17.62
...in past month	18.44	22.36	19.64	28.25	25.92	23.98	22.00	29.43
...in past week	28.03	28.77	26.13	20.23	27.08	37.02	37.94	27.88
...in past 24 hours	29.97	30.04	39.69	19.61	18.99	29.85	16.60	18.03
Frequency of Use								
...once a day +	18.44	20.27	29.13	16.58	18.23	26.30	0.00	20.13
...few times/week	27.49	30.30	28.33	21.57	35.74	39.73	38.74	24.81
...two-four times/month	24.55	26.66	24.15	29.50	24.12	18.28	32.02	42.49
...once a month or less	29.53	22.77	18.39	32.35	31.91	15.69	29.25	12.57
Ever Used								
...at home	60.06	61.31	68.99	47.33	50.05	76.52	35.51	65.08
...at work	38.76	48.20	47.87	27.99	61.16	67.30	45.72	39.90
...at school	26.26	29.78	24.51	40.02	44.12	44.19	36.56	27.25
...at other locations	24.24	38.77	32.74	22.73	48.52	54.01	25.10	36.48

Table 7d: Race and ethnicity differences over time on key web usage variables for college graduates

	White			African American			Hispanic		
	IDS2	IDS3	IDS4	IDS2	IDS3	IDS4	IDS2	IDS3	IDS4
Among all respondents with college degrees									
N	1,542	1,738	972	120	137	63	68	69	24
Current access	57.85	65.92	75.78	51.00	69.10	58.34	53.63	64.18	70.77
Ever used	43.37	56.50	70.18	33.09	55.09	53.49	42.69	56.12	67.75
Own a PC	64.65	66.81	70.21	54.09	70.43	43.60	69.01	67.23	69.66
PC access at work	63.21	65.52	70.86	76.40	74.16	70.09	70.02	62.77	75.04
Home fax	23.47	22.26	24.79	23.52	21.72	14.40	37.22	28.03	40.18
Cable	72.28	75.92	76.74	83.00	85.13	85.96	78.11	80.86	81.17
Satellite	6.49	7.29	11.34	6.40	3.76	7.83	9.47	5.59	15.22
Among Recent Web Users with College Degrees									
N	650	913	623	43	68	31	32	34	16
First Used									
...in past 2 years +	21.98	40.61	58.12	16.06	42.92	49.41	43.23	38.74	
...in past 1-2 years	21.30	24.39	20.29	41.77	23.83	19.43	0.00	22.25	
...in past year	22.80	20.85	12.13	11.68	22.19	21.69	13.65	23.90	
...in past 6 months	16.57	7.47	5.60	15.49	6.70	3.69	13.86	9.34	
...in past 3 months	17.36	6.68	3.85	15.00	4.36	5.78	29.26	5.77	
Last Used									
...in past 6 months	5.58	5.64	4.24	7.46	5.12	3.85	2.40	0.00	
...in past 3 months	12.12	10.10	5.55	26.93	12.77	5.11	7.21	6.03	
...in past month	22.68	15.29	16.27	17.19	34.77	12.56	22.16	12.58	
...in past week	24.86	28.01	28.01	24.82	23.83	41.29	33.62	21.63	
...in past 24 hours	34.76	40.96	45.93	23.60	23.51	37.19	34.61	59.76	

Frequency of Use								
...once a day +	23.67	25.78	31.32	17.92	17.92	17.92	21.51	41.94
...few times/week	27.76	31.51	31.51	21.49	25.88	35.34	45.96	25.24
...two-four times/month	24.62	23.28	21.87	23.68	32.18	29.82	5.66	26.87
...once a month or less	23.95	19.42	15.30	36.90	24.02	16.92	26.85	6.95
Ever Used								
...at home	66.47	69.01	67.52	60.75	56.83	67.92	50.22	81.26
...at work	62.69	68.00	68.51	70.15	72.38	71.52	62.34	68.28
...at school	23.53	19.86	22.23	28.39	24.05	23.20	43.67	22.02
...at other locations	24.34	31.56	28.55	33.17	35.27	37.02	36.03	24.51

By IDS 4, African Americans were more likely than whites to have ever used the Web at work, school or other locations. The percentage of African Americans who have ever used the Web at home has risen dramatically, going from 47.33 percent in IDS 2 to 76.52 percent by IDS 4. College Graduates.

Table 7d examines differences in access and use for college graduates. In IDS 2, whites had higher levels of access, usage, and home computer ownership than African Americans. In IDS 3, it appeared that these differences had disappeared. But then in IDS 4, African American rates dropped, leading to dramatic differences and larger gaps.

Thus, it appears that education does not account for the digital divide in access and usage and home PC ownership. Interestingly, both whites and African American college graduates have high levels of PC access at work and there is no gap on this variable. Outside of this finding, it is an interesting question to ask why there is such a large gap in access and usage between educated African Americans and whites. Further examination of college educated African Americans in IDS 4 is warranted.

Whites and African Americans report similar levels of recency and frequency of use, as with those with some college. Whites and African American college graduates are also equally likely to have ever used the Web from home, work, or school. However, there is a small tendency for African Americans college graduates to be more likely to have ever used the Web from other locations, and this difference has persisted over time.

Income Tables 8a and 8b show the relationship between income and Web access and usage for whites and African Americans. Not surprisingly, respondents whose household income is above the median income of $40,000 report higher levels of access, use, home computer ownership and PC access at work.

At household incomes below $40,000, whites are more likely than African Americans to have access to the Web, to have ever used the Web, and to own a home computer. The gaps in access and use may actually be increasing, although the gap in home PC ownership appears to be improving slightly. There is no difference between whites and African Americans in PC access at work at this income level.

Above the median household income of $40,000, differences between whites and African Americans in access, usage, PC ownership and PC access at work are greatly diminished compared to respondents with less household income. In IDS 2, there were significant differences in the length of time that whites and African Americans had been online. White 170.8 percent of whites had used the Internet for two years or more, only 9.08 percent of African Americans had. In contrast, African Americans were almost twice as likely as whites to be new users in IDS 2.

By IDS 4, these gaps had disappeared with over fifty percent of both African Americans and whites to have been Web users for two years or more. In IDS 2, 59.48 percent of whites, compared to 44.21 percent of African Americans were the most recent users. By IDS 4, this gap had largely disappeared, with 73.78 percent of whites and 75.22 percent of African Americans with incomes of $40,000 and over reporting they last used the Web within the past week.

Table 8a: Race and ethnicity differences over time on key web usage variables for respondents with household income below $40,000

	White			African American			Hispanic		
	IDS2	IDS3	IDS4	IDS2	IDS3	IDS4	IDS2	IDS3	IDS4
Among All Respondents with HH Income < $40,000									
N	1,967	2,472	1,315	244	381	223	164	247	69
Current access	24.67	28.69	32.92	21.68	28.13	24.98	24.98	18.73	19.45
Ever used	14.52	20.63	24.68	10.83	13.51	17.42	19.38	7.87	15.23
Own a PC	29.49	28.45	30.52	14.39	16.26	19.81	23.45	14.08	14.64
PC access at work	26.37	30.93	28.72	19.55	30.83	30.65	25.41	25.92	20.83
Home fax	6.31	6.23	7.27	3.54	2.91	6.36	5.49	4.90	6.90
Cable	63.16	66.67	68.43	60.29	67.64	75.95	60.17	62.18	57.18
Satellite	10.90	12.14	13.42	4.96	6.02	11.30	8.53	5.69	3.36

Table 8b: Race and ethnicity differences over time on key web usage variables for respondents with household income $40,000 and over

	White			African American			Hispanic		
	IDS2	IDS3	IDS4	IDS2	IDS3	IDS4	IDS2	IDS3	IDS4
Among All Respondents with Household Income $40,000+									
N	1,993	2,332	1,366	138	173	114	108	113	54
Current access	51.55	60.07	66.84	58.42	64.26	58.01	54.12	60.03	63.80
Ever used	35.66	47.78	56.51	35.60	44.92	50.36	37.66	47.77	49.68
Own a PC	62.31	61.24	63.60	64.95	63.61	61.26	55.35	62.96	54.67
PC access at work	57.78	61.28	63.02	75.32	72.40	60.48	54.38	60.89	62.11
Home fax	22.25	21.69	22.61	26.75	19.72	18.10	23.87	21.70	27.48
Cable	75.26	77.75	78.94	87.23	90.10	84.26	72.36	86.56	87.27
Satellite	11.05	12.22	14.33	9.27	9.80	12.96	8.86	11.68	16.74
Among Recent Web Users with Household Income $40,000 +									
N	753	1,063	750	57	71	56	44	49	28
First Used									
...in past 2 years +	17.08	33.70	52.00	9.08	33.13	56.29	23.26	33.47	69.24
...in past 1-2 years	20.32	25.45	19.20	26.93	21.92	21.27	8.50	17.71	7.68
...in past year	20.68	24.87	14.60	7.75	24.52	17.99	20.48	33.82	10.27
...in past 6 months	18.74	8.27	9.11	15.25	7.54	0.00	14.53	8.58	8.12
...in past 3 months	23.19	7.70	5.09	41.00	12.89	4.45	33.23	6.42	4.70

Last Used									
...in past 6 months	7.93	6.48	4.31	5.86	3.35	4.08	8.23	2.58	3.13
...in past 3 months	10.26	9.60	4.77	29.22	21.13	8.83	12.52	18.76	0.00
...in past month	22.31	17.06	17.14	20.70	31.69	11.87	24.27	15.27	18.46
...in past week	28.17	28.42	31.17	22.69	20.71	44.50	41.68	21.48	50.20
...in past 24 hours	31.31	38.43	42.61	21.52	23.13	30.72	13.30	41.91	28.21
Frequency of Use									
...once a day +	18.18	24.25	30.06	12.51	14.60	31.52	3.20	30.68	33.35
...few times/week	31.51	31.07	32.80	18.43	29.10	27.56	43.01	25.00	34.77
...two-four times/month	26.50	25.70	22.71	37.80	24.95	28.81	27.79	29.90	28.03
...once a month or less	23.81	18.98	14.43	31.26	31.36	12.11	26.01	14.42	3.86
Ever Used									
...at home	65.64	68.32	71.85	53.85	62.40	78.73	40.27	76.78	82.24
...at work	52.22	61.87	59.26	56.91	69.19	64.38	45.52	57.04	48.85
...at school	23.00	24.21	22.89	28.76	25.75	37.26	33.36	25.45	40.04
...at other locations	24.43	34.97	32.00	31.26	35.64	47.29	30.35	43.72	35.89

Gender

Tables 9a and 9b report the relationship between gender and Web access and use for whites and African Americans.Overall levels of Web access and use are lower for women than men. Among recent Web users, men are more likely to have been using the Web longer, and to have used the Web more recently. Women are more likely to be newer users. While white men are more frequent users than white women, African American men are not more frequent Web users than African American women.

White men are more likely to have access to the Web, to have ever used the Web, and to own a PC at home than African American men and these differences have persisted over time. Interestingly, the percentage of respondents who report owning a PC at home has grown for white men, but not African American men. There is a small tendency for white men to be more likely to have PC access at work.

Among recent Web users, African American men are much more likely than white men to be newer Web users and this finding persists over time. In IDS 2, white men were more than three times as likely as African American men to have been online for two years or more (20.31 percent versus 6.20 percent). By IDS 4, over fifty percent of white and African American men had been online that long. In IDS 2, white men were more likely than African American men to be the most recent Web users (65.46 percent compared to 37.04 percent). By IDS 4, both white and African American men were equally and highly likely to have used the Internet recently (75.03 percent compared to 71.37 percent, respectively).

Table 9a: Race and ethnicity differences over time on key web usage variables for men

	White			African American			Hispanic		
	IDS2	IDS3	IDS4	IDS2	IDS3	IDS4	IDS2	IDS3	IDS4
Among All Male Respondents									
N	2,045	2,465	1402	192	265	151	136	187	72
Currently	41.97	47.05	53.85	38.94	45.74	45.72	42.99	35.27	57.19
Have access									
Ever used	30.08	38.14	45.45	22.02	28.85	37.04	33.51	21.66	49.51
Own a PC	47.59	47.64	49.66	31.43	33.40	34.03	41.66	27.34	42.69
PC access at work	43.55	46.25	45.47	39.38	42.23	42.01	39.43	34.01	36.61
Home fax	16.89	15.77	16.78	12.42	9.81	10.19	17.27	10.87	21.17
Cable	68.01	73.12	74.15	64.41	77.42	78.24	69.92	67.10	76.70
Satellite	12.02	13.10	13.17	2.98	4.70	15.28	7.65	7.72	14.02
Among Male Recent Web Users									
N	714	1,042	662	55	81	53	49	55	35
First Used									
...in past 2 years +	20.31	36.90	57.44	6.20	29.56	55.37	14.51	36.69	53.65
...in past 1-2 years	20.55	24.91	18.66	17.27	19.93	19.12	4.73	21.25	16.92
...in past year	20.26	22.11	13.15	13.07	28.40	10.07	28.81	25.82	13.84
...in past 6 months	17.14	7.80	6.54	18.34	10.58	0.00	13.46	11.19	4.35
...in past 3 months	21.73	8.28	4.19	45.11	11.53	15.44	38.49	5.06	11.24

Last Used									
...in past 6 months	6.98	6.22	3.88	10.04	3.43	2.63	7.64	5.92	0.00
...in past 3 months	9.31	10.52	4.87	29.90	21.62	3.89	4.55	17.54	0.00
...in past month	18.25	16.57	16.21	23.03	22.49	22.12	32.96	18.24	27.27
...in past week	28.42	24.55	28.35	16.56	28.28	40.08	35.32	22.11	34.57
...in past 24 hours	37.04	42.14	46.68	20.48	24.18	31.29	19.53	36.20	38.18
Frequency of Use									
...once a day +	23.82	28.56	34.12	9.75	16.87	25.97	11.60	28.56	39.09
...few times/week	32.12	31.85	33.38	29.15	29.60	28.68	45.54	31.95	25.16
...two-four times/month	24.48	19.94	20.08	27.06	22.94	22.40	26.48	27.33	31.30
...once a month or less	19.58	19.65	12.42	34.04	30.59	12.95	16.37	12.16	4.46
Ever Used									
...at home	63.74	67.66	70.12	41.86	53.70	64.65	39.47	64.98	73.57
...at work	48.87	54.54	54.71	35.65	59.24	60.62	39.21	54.55	44.12
...at school	28.35	28.49	28.89	39.80	44.06	62.58	40.89	39.11	53.18
...at other locations	60.43	42.24	36.57	30.12	48.68	55.27	33.58	61.00	51.93

Table 9b: Race and ethnicity differences over time on key web usage variables for women

	White			African American			Hispanic		
	IDS2	IDS3	IDS4	IDS2	IDS3	IDS4	IDS2	IDS3	IDS4
Among All Female Respondents									
N	2,861	3,535	2,045	301	426	290	183	261	92
Currently	30.12	39.72	44.98	26.26	33.80	28.62	34.90	24.58	25.43
Have access									
Ever used	17.98	29.33	35.29	15.63	17.97	21.74	22.19	16.87	16.78
Own a PC	41.16	41.82	43.78	27.07	25.65	25.70	38.33	26.39	23.67
PC access at work	33.34	38.19	39.33	28.32	36.39	33.10	28.58	30.66	27.27
Home fax	11.35	11.74	13.02	6.56	5.28	6.57	11.79	6.65	8.63
Cable	68.87	72.65	74.82	62.58	69.31	72.98	61.92	60.77	61.28
Satellite	9.21	10.90	13.85	6.59	9.68	10.93	7.82	6.83	8.88
Among Recent Female Web Users									
N	590	973	706	49	70	64	42	41	21
First Used									
...in past 2 years +	9.74	28.03	39.31	7.58	35.41	30.29	15.57	10.11	
...in past 1-2 years	15.07	22.66	21.66	13.77	22.02	15.80	5.38	25.81	
...in past year	25.74	26.04	18.92	18.58	22.64	30.76	13.07	41.22	
...in past 6 months	21.01	11.55	11.70	18.46	7.22	13.42	31.96	13.15	
...in past 3 months	28.45	11.73	8.42	41.61	12.71	8.73	34.02	9.72	

Last Used								
...in past 6 months	10.62	9.64	7.27	11.12	6.60	1.95	10.13	2.47
...in past 3 months	16.39	13.23	8.74	32.35	20.54	20.65	17.77	11.48
...in past month	27.67	23.19	23.25	24.77	33.37	20.60	34.65	32
...in past week	27.06	29.88	32.54	22.07	21.65	30.20	27.95	26.28
...in past 24 hours	18.26	24.05	28.20	9368	17.83	26.59	9.50	27.42
Frequency of Use								
...once a day +	10.23	13.58	17.35	22.73	13.85	24.55	8.57	21.21
...few times/week	23.13	25.84	29.18	21.65	25.50	24.47	24.18	24.61
...two-four times/month	30.06	31.33	31.40	29.83	30.89	24.34	30.15	39.96
...once a month or less	36.59	29.25	22.06	25.80	29.76	26.64	37.10	17.22
Ever Used								
...at home	57.66	61.23	67.22	52.62	57.00	65.20	31.28	67.08
...at work	36.83	48.00	45.23	38.18	69.52	61.61	22.47	27.70
...at school	28.26	30.32	28.68	50.57	34.43	50.38	58.93	21.06
...at other locations	19.67	35.54	33.13	16.66	48.55	51.78	25.38	31.40

White men were also more frequent Web users than African American men in IDS 2. White men were still more likely to be more frequent Web users than African American men by IDS 4, though the difference had shrunk considerably. Over time, the percentage of African American men ever using the Web at home, work, school or other locations has increased considerably. In contrast, the percentage of white men who ever used the Web at school is flat, has grown only modestly for home and work, and has fallen for ever used at other locations. By IDS 4, African American men were more likely to have ever used the Web at school or at other locations, compared to white men.

White women are more likely than African American women to have access to the Web, to have ever used the Web, to own a PC and to have PC access at work and these differences have persisted over time. As for men, the percentage of women owning PCs at home has increased over time for white women, but not African American women. In IDS 2, African American women were much more likely than white women to be new users, but over time this difference has vanished. White women were more likely in IDS 2 than African American women to have used the Internet most recently. By IDS 4, 60.74 percent of white women, compared to 56.79 percent of African American women, had used the Internet within the past week. In contrast to previous results, African American women were more likely than white women to be the most frequent Internet users. By IDS 4, this gap had diminished with 49.02 percent of African American women, compared to 46.53 percent of white women having used the Web a few times a week or more. African American women were more likely to have ever used the Web at school or from other locations.

Tables 10a and 10b compare Web use in the presence of children in the home for whites and African Americans. Not surprisingly, overall levels of access and usage are higher for respondents who report having children under seventeen in the household. In IDS 4, whites without children at home were more likely than African Americans without children at home to have access to the Web, to have ever used the Web, to own a PC, and to have PC access at work. Some of these gaps were persistent. Among recent Web users, over fifty percent of both groups had been using the Web for two years or more by IDS 4, although African Americans without children at home were much more likely than whites to be newer users, especially in IDS 2 and IDS 4.

By IDS 4, there were few differences in recency and frequency of Web use between whites and African Americans. African Americans, were more likely to have ever used the Web at school and other locations. Children Under Seventeen.Whites were more likely to have access to the Web, to have ever used the Web, to own a PC, and slightly more likely to have PC access at work. The percentage of respondents owning a home PC, though higher for whites than African Americans, has remained constant over time.

Among recent Web users, whites with children at home were more likely to be long-term Web users and to be more recent users, but not more frequent users, compared to African Americans with children at home. Whites were also more likely to have ever used the Web at home, though this has diminished over time. African Americans were more likely to have ever used the Web at school and other locations.

Table 10a: Race and ethnicity differences over time on key web usage variables for respondents with no children under 17 in household

	White			African American			Hispanic		
	IDS2	IDS3	IDS4	IDS2	IDS3	IDS4	IDS2	IDS3	IDS4
Among All Respondents with No Kids < 17									
N	3,067	3,777	2,272	256	393	236	156	203	85
Current access	30.26	35.97	42.91	27.71	36.94	27.04	34.41	22.31	43.15
Ever used	20.47	28.32	35.39	16.18	20.56	23.67	27.12	16.59	33.60
Own a PC	36.36	36.82	40.59	19.18	25.49	24.37	33.20	22.55	33.83
PC access at work	34.15	37.54	39.69	25.56	34.67	33.29	27.44	27.76	35.18
Home fax	12.09	11.29	12.65	7.81	5.55	5.53	14.31	8.99	10.80
Cable	68.28	73.43	73.69	61.26	71.32	73.25	60.31	63.75	75.42
Satellite	9.56	11.27	12.62	2.71	5.39	12.80	7.53	5.16	6.82
Among Recent Web Users with No Kids < 17									
N	771	1,145	817	53	89	54	43	48	29
First Used									
...in past 2 years +	18.92	35.62	53.35	10.79	33.41	52.93	22.25	29.64	
...in past 1-2 years	18.17	23.51	19.05	15.04	14.11	16.10	0.00	19.33	
...in past year	23.73	24.11	14.70	15.97	33.55	13.62	25.81	41.75	
...in past 6 months	18.84	7.86	7.98	14.61	9.77	1.91	16.60	5.67	
...in past 3 months	20.34	8.90	4.93	43.59	9.16	15.44	35.54	3.61	

Last Used								
...in past 6 months	7.55	6.64	4.56	2.53	6.09	5.25	5.16	3.18
...in past 3 months	11.91	10.41	6.10	21.02	19.68	4.25	6.17	12.46
...in past month	18.41	19.77	18.30	27.68	27.37	13.62	25.76	27.06
...in past week	27.38	27.91	28.54	25.40	24.45	37.18	45.02	22.34
...in past 24 hours	34.74	35.27	42.50	23.37	22.42	39.70	17.88	34.97
Frequency of Use								
...once a day +	23.93	22.60	29.52	20.35	13.69	30.72	9.95	30.32
...few times/week	28.90	30.89	30.40	25.52	31.01	38.48	44.28	28.56
...two-four times/month	24.67	23.52	24.60	19.28	27.18	18.70	26.82	31.02
...once a month or less	22.50	22.98	15.47	34.85	28.13	12.10	18.95	10.11
Ever Used								
...at home	60.90	63.92	67.87	54.25	54.70	60.82	34.38	66.49
...at work	47.29	52.53	56.63	37.42	62.77	58.88	47.31	53.01
...at school	27.98	28.25	25.17	32.55	39.92	49.50	50.40	29.73
...at other locations	25.55	37.93	32.92	26.33	45.87	49.46	27.94	35.05

Table 10b: Race and ethnicity differences over time on key web usage variables for respondents with children under 17 in household

	White			African American			Hispanic		
	IDS2	IDS3	IDS4	IDS2	IDS3	IDS4	IDS2	IDS3	IDS4
Among All Respondents with Kids < 17									
N	1,838	2,220	1,172	237	297	205	163	245	79
Current access	44.59	54.20	59.46	36.24	41.48	45.45	42.17	35.59	36.80
Ever used	28.97 4	1.57	48.08	20.83	25.53	32.98	27.65	21.47	29.84
Own a PC	56.45	56.35	56.30	40.38	34.06	34.55	45.35	30.14	31.01
PC access at work	44.58	48.93	46.45	41.58	44.63	40.69	38.62	35.80	28.30
Home fax	16.93	17.25	18.32	10.49	9.64	10.96	14.32	8.51	17.26
Cable	68.76	72.00	75.73	65.81	74.90	77.29	70.03	63.97	62.03
Satellite	12.09	13.00	14.98	7.83	10.04	12.56	7.91	8.89	15.11
Among Recent Web Users with Kids < 17									
N	533	867	549	51	62	63	48	48	27
First Used									
...in past 2 years +	13.22	30.55	44.81	3.94	30.24	36.82	10.26	25.67	
...in past 1-2 years	18.66	24.30	21.16	16.30	28.11	18.63	8.24	25.26	
...in past year	20.98	23.48	16.82	15.03	17.86	24.14	19.70	24.15	
...in past 6 months 18.45	11.02	9.81	21.08	8.64	9.45	24.41	16.10		
...in past 3 months	28.69	10.65	7.40	43.65	15.15	10.77	37.38	8.81	

Last Used								
...in past 6 months	9.32	8.78	6.34	16.17	3.18	0.00	10.99	5.66
...in past 3 months	12.28	12.91	7.14	37.99	22.85	17.17	12.77	17.27
...in past month	25.73	19.04	20.54	20.99	26.29	27.63	38.79	20.87
...in past week	28.43	25.74	32.13	14.29	26.91	34.38	23.89	24.47
...in past 24 hours	24.24	33.54	33.85	10.56	20.77	20.82	13.56	31.73
Frequency of Use								
...once a day +	12.64	21.74	23.44	11.83	17.88	21.06	10.54	23.10
...few times/week	28.26	27.64	32.97	26.21	24.58	27.32	31.38	29.85
...two-four times/month	28.62	26.15	25.61	36.49	24.89	26.91	28.84	30.59
...once a month or less	30.28	24.46	17.97	27.48	32.65	24.71	29.25	16.47
Ever Used								
...at home	61.79	66.02	69.99	40.89	55.39	60.84	37.01	65.24
...at work	40.79	51.03	43.26	36.24	64.03	62.77	22.25	39.39
...at school	28.67	30.32	32.90	52.80	40.47	63.08	47.41	34.48
...at other locations	26.93	40.86	37.45	23.01	51.72	57.05	31.79	60.43

Web Shopping

The rate of searching for information on the Web and purchasing products on the Web is increasing over time. In IDS 2, whites were more likely to use the Web to purchase a product or service online. In IDS 3 and IDS 4, whites were also more likely to purchase online, but the gap is closing. However, in IDS 2, both whites and African Americans were equally likely to search for product information online. Yet in IDS 3 and IDS 4, whites are more likely than African Americans to have searched the Web for product information. Potential explanations of the differences in search behavior are that African-Americans are less interested in comparing products and services online, are obtaining this information from other sources, or are simply finding less of interest to search for online.

Internet users ranked business opportunities as a relatively unimportant reason for current Internet users, but a very important reason for non-users. This was phrased, however, in terms of "making money." Table 12 shows business uses of the Web among recent Web users with access to a PC at work.

As with Web shopping variables, items in IDS 2 are not comparable to items in IDS 3 and IDS 4, so no direct comparisons may be made from IDS 2 to IDS 3 or IDS 2 to IDS 4. In IDS 2, whites were more likely than African Americans to use the Web to research competitors, publish product information, sell products and services, for customer service and support and for vendor support and communication. In IDS 3, a number of these race differences in business uses of the Web have gone away and some new differences emerged.

For example, whites were more likely than African Americans to use the Web for internal communication, and still more likely to use the Web for customer service support and vendor support and communication. By IDS 4, African Americans were, for the first time, more likely than whites to have access to an Intranet at work, to use the Web for internal communication, and for customer service and support. However, whites were more likely to use the Web to buy products or services. It is likely that these differences may reflect different job functions.

The role of access to the Internet at home needs to be much more clearly understood. Whites are more likely to have access to the Internet and to have ever used the Web than African Americans and these gaps appear to be increasing over time. By IDS 4, in most cases there were no or only slight differences between whites and African Americans in how recently they had used the Web, how frequently, or in their length of time online. Gaps in general Web access and use between African-Americans and whites appear to be driven by whether or not there is a computer present in the home. Access to a personal computer, whether at home, work, school or somewhere else, is important because it is currently the dominant mechanism by which individuals can access the Internet. Formal coursework was the least often mentioned way people were introduced to the Internet. Long term Internet users were most likely to have learned at work; for recent Internet users, friends/family and self-taught were equally important. These results reinforce the importance of the presence of a computer at home, or the opportunity to access the Web from locations other than the home, in stimulating Web use.

Insight into the importance of reducing this gap in Web use between whites and African-Americans is provided by Anderson and Melchior's discussion of information redlining. Information redlining signifies the relegation of minorities into situations where satisfying their information needs is weighed against their economic and social worth. From the minority point of view, this is both an access issue and a form of discrimination.

The new technologies of information are not simply tools of private communication as a telephone is, or tools of entertainment as a television is. They provide direct access to information sources that are essential in making social choices and keeping track of developments not only in the world at large, but also within their immediate neighborhoods. Unless the neighborhoods are properly served, there is no way out of information redlining for most of these disadvantaged groups.

In addition to gaps in home computer ownership, the implications of differential Internet access at locations outside the home, including school, the workplace and other locations needs to be clearly understood. Additional access points stimulate usage. Research is necessary to understand the impact of multiple access points on Web use, particularly for individuals who have no access at home. Public-private initiatives such as Bell Atlantic's efforts in Union City and Bill Gates announcement of a $200 million gift to provide library access to the Internet are a step in the right direction. It has also been noted that "community networks and public access terminals offer great potential for African-American communities". Further, the recent roll-out of E-rate funds provides a significant opportunity for researchers to understand the factors important in stimulating Web usage among those least likely to have access.

The role of Web access in the schools, compared to other locations, needs to be clearly understood. Students enjoy the highest levels of Internet access and Web use, especially when there are computers in their households. However, white students are still more likely than African American students to have access and to use the Internet, and these gaps persist over time.

Access to technology does not make much sense unless people are properly educated in using the technologies. Understanding the differences in Internet access and use among all racial and ethnic groups in the United States is required for a comprehensive understanding of technology adoption and its impact on the digital economy. Subsequent studies need to oversample members of minority groups. This is required so that there will be sufficient numbers of all minority groups to perform post-stratification adjustments to create weights that yield population-projectable results for each minority group.

Reasons for the gap between African-Americans and whites in Web search behavior need to be clearly understood. Such differences could have important implications for the ultimate success of commercial efforts online. White Web users are more likely to report searching for product or service-related information than African Americans.

Whites are more likely to search for information online than are African Americans. More generally, consumer behavior in the commercial Web environment is complex and only weakly understood. Further research is needed to explore fully the differences in consumer behavior on the Web and their implications for commercialization.

Studies investigating the extent of multicultural content on the Web are needed. Another possibility for the gap between African-Americans and whites in Web search behavior is that there is insufficient content of interest to African-Americans. Interactive Marketing News claimed that "while there are about 10 million sites on the Web, there are fewer than 500 sites targeted" to African-Americans. However, others have commented on the multicultural diversity of the Web.

Household income explains race differences in Internet access, use, home computer ownership and PC access at work. In terms of overall access and use, higher household income positively affects access to a computer. But at lower incomes, gaps in access and use between whites and African Americans existed and were increasing. Research is necessary to determine the efforts most likely to be effective to ensure access for lower-income Americans, especially African Americans.

5

Educational Constraints

The speed with which the revolution in information and communication technology (ICT) has taken place is phenomenal. The changes the ICT revolution has wrought are not limited to one single sector of society, nor do they just add another column in the aggregate tables of macro-economists. The impact of the ICT revolutions provide modern illustrations of Says's law: Supply creates its own demand.

The way the hardware of ICT was produced and operated has itself become one of the foremost expressions of globalization; components come from all continents-chips from Asia, software from America, mobile phones from Europe. Brand names have instant recognition around the world: Acer, Sony, Intel, Microsoft, and Nokia. On the other hand, satellites orbiting the globe allow for instant communication on an unprecedented scale.

The development of new products and services was part of a vast distributed and yet integrated global division of labour, whether it was in the development of new for-profit products and services or the more altruistic open-source contributions from a diverse crowd of enthusiasts.

The new links-the Internet and the World Wide Web-became the first truly dynamic and interactive network that individuals could access from all over the world. Much of what is on the Web is not mass communication in the classical sense: one source, one way, many users. It is by and for interacting people. Indeed, in many respects individuals were ahead of institutions in realizing the Web's potential. For example, music was swapped via the Internet before it became commoditized.

The ICT revolution has been very much about spotting opportunities and inviting everybody to learn to make good use of them. Indeed, the ICT revolution is perhaps above all else a revolution in learning. Individuals have seen the potential of the new tools and introduced them into their homes on a vast scale. Firms have applied them to an ever-widening range of activities: bookkeeping, production control, management, communication, marketing, and drug development. Public authorities have incorporated them into all of their activities, from vaccination programs to tracking criminals.

The first revolution started during World War II, with the first large, automatic, general electromechanical calculator, Harvard Mark. It was 50 feet long, eight feet tall, and weighed five tons. A couple of years later, ENIAC was presented in Philadelphia, based on radio tubes and practically without any internal memory, yet using 18,000 vacuum tubes and weighing 30 tons. Each time a new task was to be performed, some 6,000 switches covering three walls had to be thrown. In 1947, the first transistor, and, on its basis, faster and more powerful computers were constructed. Computers became a new catchword, and input-output technology graduated from punch cards to magnetic tape, faster printers, and more languages for programming. Applications also were expanded, from use in academic research to weather forecasting, from airline ticketing to accounting. This development continues; the first ICT revolution is still under way.

The second ICT revolution has its roots in the 1970s, when the first "processors on a chip" and magnetic discs were constructed. But as late as 1977, Ken Olson, the legendary president of the computer company, Digital, stated: "There is no reason anyone would want a computer in their home." He was definitely wrong. In the same year, Steve Jobs and Steve Wosniak started to sell their Apple II, and Bill Gates and Paul Allen had already founded a firm called Microsoft. From being an esoteric toy, the personal computer gradually became a valuable tool for word processing, accounting, and, after a while, pictures. IBM, which at first grossly underestimated the markets for the personal computer (PC), launched its first machine under that name in 1981. Now the PC has become as widespread as the radio when grandparents were young-indeed, as widespread as bicycles are among today's youth. This second ICT revolution continues like the first: the capacities of the machines increase, their applications expand, and the number of people who use them multiplies.

The third ICT revolution is that microprocessors have become embedded in an ever-widening range of products: the steering systems of airplanes, the control panels of hydroelectric power stations, domestic air conditioning systems, the traffic lights in streets. Even when we do not recognize it, they have become part of everyday lives: in video players, credit cards, remote controllers, cameras, hotel room door locks, and smart buildings. There is a microprocessor embedded in digital scale in the bathroom. If you use an electric toothbrush, its functions are governed by some 3,000 lines of programming. Microprocessors translate bar codes into prices at the cash register, monitor electronic injection of fuel in cars, and determine where the elevator stops in building. An ordinary household now contains some 100 microprocessors, in everything from dishwashers to alarm systems. Microprocessors constantly expand their capacity, applications, and users.

The fourth ICT revolution stretches back to the late 1960s, when the US Department of Defense drew up guidelines for a communication network among computers (ARPANET). After a while, universities in and outside the United States were hooked up to it, and some started to use it to send messages. France developed its variant-its Minitel system-at the beginning of the 1980s, at the same time the U.S. National Science Foundation set up its own network among academic institutions that later became part of Internet. A dozen universities on the U.S. East Coast with IBM mainframes contributed with BITNET. In Europe, EARN became a network among academic institutions, while CERN in Geneva was crucial in the development of the World Wide Web, which got its name in 1990. A couple of years later, surfing on the 'net started, and more and more people hooked up. A PC needed a modem to use its potential fully. This fourth ICT revolution continues like the others as more and more computers are interlinked with an ever-growing number of "servers" and an expanding range of applications. Yet, the most important part of the fourth ICT revolution was this: on the computer networks engineers had constructed, users built social networks to make them useful and effective-in this case, the social superstructure built on the material basis became really super.

The fifth ICT revolution was linking without lines-the new possibilities opened by mobile phones. At first, they were big and bulky. Reduction in size and weight was accompanied by expansion of reach and functions, and miniaturization was accompanied by multifunctionality. Mobile phones could be used not just for talking, but also to exchange messages, receive news or stock exchange quotes, review restaurants, or order movie tickets. Phones are no longer only for transmitting phonemes; now they can transmit written messages, pictures, and music. Linking without lines now takes place not just intercontinentally via satellites, but also via high-frequency short-range radio transmitters covering a specific area or cell and inside buildings by "Bluetooth" and infrared light.

Educational Potential of ICTs

Since the ICT revolution is a revolution in learning, it also has transformed available technologies, the means and methods of studying, the modalities of school operations, the manner of investment and expenditure of resources, and the very way think about what education could be and should do. Even before the Internet became a new mode of communication, and the World Wide Web made it possible to access learning material anywhere, universities had started to use telecommunications and computers for teaching. But with the advent of the Internet and the Web, these opportunities have expanded vastly, and educational institutions have made more and more varied use of them. Course material is posted on the Web, assignments can be communicated through the 'net, and teachers can be accessed around the clock by the new modes of transmission. The new education programs have reached out to off-campus students, often from long distances, but they also have reached in to regular students in novel ways by providing learning materials in new forms. They include a wide spectrum, from French grammar to fractal geometry, from guides to trilobites to flash cards for physics. The Internet also changes the ways schools work by making possible closer cooperation and interaction among them, within the same country and across continents and oceans. One example is joint "virtual projects." Likewise, parents can be kept informed via the Websites of schools-virtual PTAs, so to speak.

Not only has ICT transformed the way learning institutions work, it also has changed the organized education. ICT has become a medium in the original sense of the word: something in the middle, between the substance to be learned and the student who is to master it. First, it liberates provision of education from the constraints of time and place: many courses can be accessed from more or less anywhere and at any time. Second, training can be customized, by allowing material to be adapted to individual levels and tasks to be paced according to personal progress. But tailored capacity and development does not mean that students cannot interact-individualized does not mean isolated.

To the contrary, the physical network allows students to work together, whether for mutual consultation and advice or support and encouragement.

Hence, the new education technologies alter the means and modes of studying. Students can link to other students, across boundaries and across continents. Children can take part in the development of learning materials for each other in other classrooms or countries. Teachers in the remotest places can be encouraged to take part in important professional development projects. Indeed, the whole education system can work like a neural network, where cells with synapses to other cells can fire them up. The Internet also can become a network for altruism. Institutionally, so much on the Web is there for free and for all. A large part of the available educational resources is created by groups outside of schools and academic institutions, yet is free for all and provides excellent inputs for learning. Sometimes, such worldwide community service is well organized, such as the scanning, typing, or proofreading of classical texts that are entered on Websites open to all, or when the classification of craters on Mars is set up as voluntary work among informed amateurs linked by the Internet. Individually, some communities have experimented with tutors mentoring students from home. Such acts of generosity allow those participating in them to engage their minds and help others; it sure beats the millions of clicks wasted on solitaire.

The ICT revolution offers new intrinsic opportunities; it dramatically changes what can be learned and by whom as well as what can be produced and provided by whom. These potential changes, however, pose many new challenges for educational planners. These challenges can be divided into two broad types: those that pertain to equity and those that pertain to quality. But unless educational planners respond to these changes and challenges with commensurate speed, they will become, so to speak, technologically challenged. Although in many Western countries, the majority of households have PCs linked to the Internet, considerable differences remain along regional and class lines. Several studies document that boys are more active than girls in using the new technical tools. And though schools also are increasingly well equipped and connected, standards vary within countries with educational level and type. The same applies to teacher training and skills. This raises the broader question of equity: within countries as well as between countries, particularly between the industrialized and developing world. It is true that millions of PCs are sold every year and millions gain access to the Internet.

Similarly, there are great differences between corporate actors, public as well as private, in their capacity to become-to use the current jargon-"net-based education providers." Many countries have adopted ICT policies for their education systems that cover not only hardware and infrastructure, but educational materials available for schools and students as well. Such materials, increasingly available on the Internet, range from mathematics resources in Norway to lists of recommended books for California's schools. They can be accessed freely by both domestic and foreign users. In addition, many teachers and professional associations make their best work available free for anyone to use. For example, a simple search for the "Pythagorean theorem" on the Web yields more than 10,000 sites, many of which make available all kinds of useful material-e.g., animated proofs that are much easier to follow than their textbook equivalents. In this sense, the Internet is the greatest venue for exchange of educational good deeds ever constructed.

Education equals finance-public funds to be spent and private demand to be targeted. Hence ICT, and particularly the Internet, is not only an arena for altruism and experiments, but also for business, entrepreneurship, and, sometimes, exploitation. In other words, education is increasingly becoming a market, and a global one at that. In a market, there are customers and producers. And access to the production side of this market is even less equitable than access to its usage side. Some nations also actively promote programs for foreigners by distance education via the Internet. Australia is a prominent example, where services from its educational institutions have grown into a whole export industry. This is a very interesting and, in many respects, auspicious development, but it also raises a whole range of questions for educational planners about quality, certification, and accreditation. It is notable that the World Trade Organization is considering proposals to add the import and export of higher education courses to its protocols on services marketed internationally; "education products" can then be traded as a commodity from one country to another. This development provides further opportunities for students. It releases education from national control, and it makes the market a stronger force in the globalization of education. On the other hand, planners and officials in developing or smaller countries may face an expanding international market with powerful actors and many new ventures about which they have imperfect knowledge, exercise scant control, and have few possibilities for participation.

Thus, the issue of equity pertaining to ICT has to be addressed along two dimensions: equitable access of students as consumers, where the poorer peoples and nations are put at a disadvantage; and equitable provision of content, where the poor are even worse off. Ideally, one wishes for equal opportunity to participate. But access for different actors-both as users and producers-is weighted by their resources. Hence, initial differences are often reproduced, reinforced, and even magnified. A formidable challenge, therefore, continues to face planners of international education: how to define the problem and provide assistance for development.

As ICT is rapidly becoming an integral part of the social environment and jobs are being transformed rapidly into tapping on keyboards and looking at screens, traditional literacy is no longer sufficient—what could be called, 'Iteracy,' becomes imperative. Learning to work a PC and surfing the Internet is becoming crucial for functioning in the workplace, for effective citizenship, for entertainment, and for personal growth. With the rapid change in technology, training cannot be a one-shot affair; we have to be updated continuously to stay abreast of developments. Planning and designing educational systems so that they familiarize students with a technology that is being modified and evolving continuously is not just an intellectual challenge, it is also an economic one.

This problem is exacerbated by the fact that many vendors of new technologies are sometimes more pushers than providers, promoting solutions that have a short useful life or little compatibility with what emerge as industry standards. The history of information technology is not just a history of innovation but also a history of misguided investments. This situation applies to hardware as well as to "learning packages" and software that promise more than is delivered. What is bought is often expensive and inappropriate, resulting in costly mistakes, not just in economic terms, but in terms of time stolen from students who would have been better off using more proven methods of learning. Sometimes new solutions are pushed by politicians and ministers as well: they feel they need to prove they are "modern" by going for gadgets, but they are out of office when the negative results are in. Moreover, it takes time to discover where the potential of ICT in education can best be tapped, and as technology itself is changing, final solutions will continue to evade us.

The learning process also may be skewed in unfortunate directions. Much is made of the fact that ICT has become increasingly "interactive." Learning programs can be tailored to each student, learning at his or her own pace, and being introduced to more challenging tasks as learning proceeds. However, interaction in learning cannot be restricted to per-son-machine relations; person-person relations will always remain crucial. In industrialized countries, no previous generation of children has had so little contact and communication with the world of adults. Learning has become more age-graded, as has all social interaction. TV, videogames, and Internet-provided pictures and music draw the young into a more virtual world. Hence, rather than formal education also placing students increasingly in front of a screen, planners must be concerned that students are engaged in more real than virtual interaction and connected to actual adults rather than just to their products. Children and youth need positive feedback from applets, but they also need to be seen and respected by peers and grownups as real people. What holds for the educational process also holds for educational content. Demand-driven education means, increasingly, education that is "just in time" and "just enough." Learning what is deemed not immediately relevant may be discarded as definitely wasted. But this concept of knowledge and skills is a perversion, even of a utilitarian justification of it. It is a perversion of the rationale for a broad liberal arts education where the goal is not just to enable one to solve a problem at hand but to develop abilities as a human being to perceive and to participate, to experience, to empathize, and to excel. But then the whole diversity of one's talents must be nurtured and developed. Education, after all, means to "lead out," within and beyond one's present confines, by bringing out latent abilities and talents.

There is another issue with demand-driven education as it is commonly practiced. The growth in knowledge does not just generate a steady stream of new facts, findings, and products—about viruses, proteins, or superconductors. It also means that older knowledge becomes superseded. For instance, it is no longer useful to know which electronic vacuum tubes could be used in a computer. But new facts and data do not only mean that knowledge may become obsolete. They also mean that certain types of established knowledge become more important.

Even from a purely utilitarian view, "just in time" and "just enough" knowledge is misguided. First, it takes knowledge to know what you need to know. Second, truly new insights are often the result of serendipity-the happy chance combination of seemingly unconnected ideas to a new conception. "Just in time" knowledge is, in practice, often too late, and "just enough" knowledge often makes you miss the critical piece to solve the big puzzle. Educational planners have to consider what a well-rounded education is. The whole point of education as a common human enterprise is that no student can bring out his or her potential if left to the student's own haphazard personal search. Students have to be led out, "educated" in the original sense of the word.

ICT does not suit all students, all subjects, or all phases of learning equally well. There are already considerable differences say, between the offerings in mathematics and history compared to those in music and physical education. Much depends on how ICT-assisted learning is done, and, as in traditional teaching, there are no fast formulas. Discovering and developing the potential of ICT will surely take time, and what we find may not be valid for all time because the context surely will change. Technology in itself is not a panacea; uploading Web content in different subjects does not in itself result in quality teaching or effective use. Teachers have to be trained and need to feel knowledgeable and skilled-not always easy in an environment where young students are often quicker than their teachers to learn new technologies.

On the other hand, the lack of willingness to mobilize the young to learn from one another—in the same way as they learn the tricks of new video games—is not only old-fashioned but even counterproductive. Educational planners can focus no longer just on how to secure implementation; they need to arrange for continuous experimentation and innovation to learn by doing in an ever-changing environment where even what is being learned and done is changing. There are optimistic theories about development-about a great technological leap forward or about latecomers' ability to leapfrog generations of already outdated technologies. Yet, the digital divide will be with us for years to come, and the poor will remain in the worst position for a long time, even under the most ambitious programs.

Social, economic, and technological changes of the past decades are making education and training for all more crucial than ever. Yet, educational systems, to different degrees worldwide, are struggling to afford educational opportunities for all, to provide their graduates with the necessary knowledge and skills for evolving marketplaces and sophisticated living environments, and to prepare citizens for lifelong learning. To meet these challenges, countries have to focus concurrently on expanding access, improving internal efficiency, promoting the quality of teaching and learning, and improving system management.

Some countries and institutions have turned to ICTs and are exploring ways by which ICTs may help them in pursuing their educational goals. As Table 1 illustrates, one technology may have different potentials depending on the purpose for using it. Many of the technologies have similar characteristics. Therefore assessments of the potential and appropriateness of particular technologies must be based on educational needs and objectives, rather than on the technologies themselves.

Table 1

ICTs and their Potential for Education

Technology	*Outreach*	*Flexibility*	*Sensorial Stimulation*	*Interactivity*
Radio	High	Limited	Audio only	Limited
Television	High	Limited	Audiovisual	Limited
Video	Low	High	Audiovisual	Limited
PC	Low	High	Audiovisual	High
Internet	Highest	High	Audiovisual	Highest

Expanding access to education is a matter of both economic development and social justice. It is true that worldwide illiteracy rates have declined in the past 30 years, but it is also true that the demands on knowledge are much higher now than 30 years ago. In the past, an agrarian society could thrive economically even when more than half of its population was barely literate, but this is no longer possible in modern societies in the Information Age. To remain economically competitive and prosper in this global. In many countries, whose budgets already are stretched thin, expanding access to education under traditional models is not an option.

Dramatic conflicts and the burgeoning HIV/AIDS crisis in many countries have disrupted social services, including education, and diverted resources that could be used to maintain, let alone, expand educational opportunity. Public expenditure on education already represents 25% of total government expenditures. The country's illiteracy rate for youth aged 15-24 is close to 30% for both genders (45% for girls). A program to eliminate illiteracy that relies on constructing more schools and hiring more teachers will require a level of public investment in Togo that may deplete the country's budget, leaving other essential services unattended.

For more than a century, education has used technology to expand beyond the physical limits of schools and university campuses and reach more and nontraditional groups of students. For instance, in the beginning of the last century, Australia and New Zealand used a system of itinerant teachers to educate children and youth living in sparsely inhabited territories. The teachers maintained contact with their students through postal correspondence.

Radio, television, and computer-related technologies have expanded outreach potential further, and higher education institutions have been at the forefront of this expansion. In 1992, 41% of higher education students in Thailand and 38% in Turkey studied at a distance. The China TV University System (Republic of China) and Anadolu University in Turkey each serves more than 500,000 students per year. The United Kingdom Open University has provided education to more than 2 million individuals since it was established about 30 years ago.

Distance learning institutions generally use a mix of technologies that may include printed material, videos, video-conferencing, CD-ROMs, e-mail, and the Internet. Many of them start with less expensive technologies, such as printed materials, and move to faster and more powerful resources as the need for expansion increases. The Open University of Hong Kong is an example of this movement.

Expanding access also means integrating populations that have been traditionally excluded from education for cultural and social reasons. In cultures with strict rules regarding interaction between genders, girls may be forced to leave school before puberty to avoid contact with male colleagues and teachers. For girls who remain in school, the rules regarding with whom they may or may not talk make it difficult to succeed. If a girl is having academic difficulties, she may rather fail than address the male teacher. Technology can promote alternatives for educating women that are more cost-effective than all-female schools without disrupting cultural traditions.

Television and radio broadcasts or Internet-based technologies enable girls to continue their studies from home or small learning centers. Technology functions as a neutral mediator, without gender or cultural allegiances, thereby facilitating communication. An essay exercise in a co-educational class at the African Nazarene University that required the use of computers illustrates the potential of ICTs to overcome barriers in communication. Faced with the challenge of learning a new technology, the students forgot tribal rivalries and gender differences to exchange information and work side by side. For persons with disabilities-who represent another significant and forgotten sector of the world population-technologies provide essential supports enabling them to participate in the educational system and the job market. VisualTek is a camera and monitor that enlarge print materials for people with visual disabilities. Voice synthesizers enable individuals with muscular dystrophies to communicate. Special computer software can be used to ameliorate learning disabilities or to enhance the memory of individuals with traumatic brain injury. Keyboard adaptations enable individuals with motor disabilities to write, and the Internet can connect homebound individuals to classrooms and workplaces. Lifelong learning and economic development for populations living outside mainstream cultures are two other venues for using ICTs.

A multilingual database catalogue offers the artisans' work to a worldwide customer base. The network receives and fills orders and is responsible for quality control. Currently, the Virtual Souk involves more than 700 artisans in Morocco, Tunisia, and Lebanon. Business organizations are investing heavily in distance learning technologies, particularly Internet-based applications, to train managers and employees while avoiding the costs and disruptions related to travel. The Ford Motor Company spent $100 million on a training network using interactive satellite technology that transmits up to eight live training sessions at a time to any of the 5,000 Ford dealerships across the United States.

The internal efficiency of an educational system is measured by its ability to deliver quality education in cost-effective ways. The traditional model for providing primary through tertiary education, adopted across the world, relies on three basic principles. There must be a predetermined path, divided into grades, that leads to a diploma, and students must follow this path, regardless of their interests, needs, or abilities. There must be a hierarchic structure where the instructor is the provider of knowledge and the students are the recipients.

The traditional school is, therefore, a physical entity organized into classrooms where learners congregate according to a grade structure and constrained by the limits of space and time. If a school serves students from grades 1 through 12, it must have at least 12 classrooms to accommodate each grade separately. Each classroom must have one teacher. A certain number of teachers require a principal and, often, administrative and teaching support. If the number of students or grades increases, so must the number of needed classrooms, teachers, and support personnel. Generally, beginning in the seventh grade, another dimension is added to the classroom/grade framework: specialization. From then on, the number of teachers is related to both the number of classrooms and the number of specialties offered. Each school must have at least one mathematics teacher, a science teacher, a social studies teacher, and so on.

As the educational level advances, classroom organizations will rely more on specialization than grades, but the framework is maintained. To be cost-effective within this structure, the learning place must have a critical number of students that justifies school construction and maintenance, particularly personnel costs. In areas of low population density, building and maintaining schools to serve the traditional paradigm is economically prohibitive. The requirement of one specialist per specialty makes secondary schools an even more expensive venture. Some countries sidestep the problem by leaving the solution to individual families, with catastrophic results. If the families choose to move to urban areas and ensure their children's education, they jeopardize their country's fragile economic balance and further deplete the economy of their native regions. If they decide to remain, they jeopardize their children's future. Areas of high population density but weak economy are not free of problems. In this case, the traditional model encourages administrators to accommodate as many students as possible in one classroom to control personnel costs, which leads to over-crowded and unsafe environments that are unfit for learning.

The capacity of ICTs to reach students in any place and at any time has the potential to promote revolutionary changes in the traditional educational paradigm. First, it eliminates the premise that learning time equals classroom time. To avoid overcrowded classrooms, a school may adopt a dual-shift system without reducing its students' actual study time. Students may attend school for half a day and spend the other half involved in educational activities at home, in a library, at work, or in another unconventional setting. They may be required to watch an educational radio/television program and complete related activities, or work on a computer-assisted lesson at the school technology lab or in a community learning center. For areas with low population density, multigrade schools become viable alternatives. While more advanced students listen to an educational program on the radio or watch a television broadcast, the teacher can attend to the students who are in less advanced levels or vice versa. Latin America began experimenting with television to bring education to rural, low-population areas as early as the 1960s.

In 1964, the Mexican government tried television as an alternative to provide secondary education (grades 7-9) for children in rural communities. Telesecundaria was created to respond to the needs of rural areas where a general secondary school (grades 7-9) was not feasible, because there were not enough students and it was difficult to attract teachers. A quarter-century later, Telesecundaria has become a success story about the power of television to expand access and improve education in cost-effective ways.

Traditional educational systems also tend to rely on curricula that were developed at the beginning of the Industrial Revolution and are now disconnected from the realities of the job market. For bright students, these systems offer little in the way of motivation. Eventually, a few extraordinary students will be able to skip a grade, but rushing through the system is not encouraged, and early graduates may find obstacles when they attempt to gain access to the next level. For low-income students, who have less academic support, the schools offer even less: the wealthier schools lure the best teachers, leaving the least prepared for schools in poor and remote areas. When the need to work conflicts with schools' requirements, the student sees no reason to stay in school. As a result, these systems perpetuate social inequalities, lose many excellent students to boredom, increase the costs of education through high dropout rates and grade retention, and pass on to employers or other systems the costs of retraining their graduates.

ICTs have the potential to bring the products of the best teachers to classrooms anywhere in the world. For self-motivated, disciplined students, ICTs can speed the path toward a degree and expand their learning options through self-study. Students can shop courses on the Internet and choose their own program of study and schedules. Students in virtual schools can take extra online courses to graduate earlier or fulfill specific interests and curiosity. For those who need to balance studies with work and family obligations-full- or part-time workers, parents of small children, homebound individuals-this flexibility may be most cost-effective for them. The management of distance learning is not without difficulty, and, in many cases, local regulations function as obstacles to innovations. However, the demand for more and specialized education is encouraging new arrangements that rely on ICTs to establish communication networks among partner institutions and facilitate student-centered, rather than program-centered organizations, such as the University of the Highlands and Islands. Research on brain physiology and cognitive psychology is challenging the traditional model of learning as mastery of facts and concepts. Thoughts, feelings, dreams, and imagination are equally involved in the complex phenomenon that is human nature. Perception, for instance, includes at least two basic components:

— an objective component mediated through the senses, which provide the brain with information about the objects surrounding us, their descriptions and location, and position in relation to them; and

— a subjective component that analyzes the perceived objects through the lens of personal experiences and idiosyncrasies, previous knowledge, and cultural biases.

Images are key components of the process of acquiring and using information because of their ability to condense large amounts of data. Research on working memory proposes that information is stored as images in visuospatial sketch-pads to be used later. The process involves both imageries-the mental reconstructions of objects no longer present to senses, and imagination-the mental construction of unknown objects. In addition to their role in retention and recall, images have the ability to decode unfamiliar symbols into known representations, a helpful function in language acquisition.

Textbook images traditionally have been used in foreign language classes with this decoding function. Images are equally important in the acquisition of science and mathematics, which, similar to a foreign language, have their own symbols, terminologies, and grammatical structures. Although definitions of quality learning may disagree on details, it is generally accepted that, for learning to occur, the learners must be motivated, basic concepts must be understood, and knowledge must be advanced through more complex, higher-order thinking skill tasks. As we move away from linear learning, we get closer to how the brain functions.

ICTs diversify the systems of representation through the use of various types of stimuli (images, sound, and movement) and address the needs of diverse types of learning (visual, psychomotor, and affective). In addition, ICTs have the potential to enhance educational quality by increasing motivation, facilitating acquisition of basic skills, promoting inquiry and exploration, and preparing individuals for the technology-driven world.

An effective teaching/learning process must stimulate intellectual curiosity and offer a sense of enjoyment that will move the students from the passive role of recipients of information to the active role of builders of knowledge. Yet, engaging the learner in this process can be the most challenging task for teachers. ICTs are effective instructional aides to engage students in the learning process. Videos, television, and computer multimedia software provide information that can be authentic and challenging in addition to stimulating students' sensorial apparatus through images, color, sound, and movement.

A training program for bank clerks in the United States was unable to offer on-the-job training because banks refused to accept trainees without some experience. The instructors decided to use videos of actual clerks working at a local bank and trainees role-playing clerk-customer situations. Trainees watched the movies and discussed the tasks involved, potential problems, preferred solutions, and their weaknesses/ strengths. After the videos were introduced, the program placement rates increased from 70% to 93% over a two-year period. Although radio programs do not have the visual appeal of television or computer, Interactive Radio Instruction (IRI) uses songs, drama-like plots, and comic situations to attract and maintain the attention of students of all ages in rural and low-income areas of developing countries.

Transmission of accumulated knowledge to new generations is an essential component of the educational process. This includes basic skills and information that are at the foundation of more complex knowledge. It would be inefficient to use a time-consuming process, such as inquiry and exploration, to transmit basic information. In addition, nonstructured learning environments based solely on inquiry and exploration may be confusing and overwhelming for some children and youth. These students will do better in well-structured classrooms, where the information is broken into less complex units, thus making it easier to understand. Exposition and practice strategies help to structure the classroom, enhance retention and recall, and cut learning time.

Computers have three attributes that make them powerful aides for drill and practice strategies: large memory, speed, and the capacity to repeat the same task an infinite number of times without reducing performance. In addition, they provide students with the opportunity to learn on their own time and at their own pace. Computer-aided instruction (CAI) has been used successfully in different settings for basic skill instruction. CAI programs are divided into modules that maintain a hierarchy of concepts and skills. The students have to master each module before being allowed to move to the next, more complex level. An evaluation at the end of each module gives the students immediate feedback. If they respond correctly to a determined percentage of questions, they advance. Otherwise, they repeat the module or enter remedial units until the skills or concepts are mastered. The program can keep a history of the students' performance-lessons learned, topics with which the student had more difficulty, strategies that improved learning, and how many times the student had to repeat the module.

With this information, the teacher can develop an individualized plan that addresses each student's specific weaknesses and strengths. CAI was introduced as an aid in mathematics classes, but it is now used for different disciplines, grade levels, and objectives. The military has used CAI in training for a long time. Overall, research shows that when CAI is applied well, users learn faster, retain more, and tend to have a more positive attitude toward learning than students receiving traditional instruction. Computers also can be used as auxiliary tools in mathematics and science classes to free teachers' and students' time. While computers work on repetitive tasks (such as long calculations and statistical computations), teachers and students can concentrate on analytical activities that require higher-order thinking skills. Research indicates that elementary and secondary school students who use calculators have higher test scores and better attitudes toward mathematics than their peers who do not use calculators. Elementary school children who use computers and calculators in the classroom were found to understand mathematical concepts much earlier than expected.

Although basic skills and information are essential components of the teaching/learning process, learning is more than information transfer. Learning requires the ability to analyze and synthesize information, use it in diverse circumstances, and propose new lines of inquiry that foster knowledge. Inquiry and exploration are essential strategies to attain those abilities. ICTs have the potential to restore curiosity to education. ICTs can take students on exciting journeys through time and space. Movies, videos, audio technology, and computer animations bring sound and movement to static textbook lessons and enliven children's reading classes. They also provide social studies and foreign language students with vicarious experiences of distant societies and bygone times. Spreadsheets can store and analyze large amounts of data necessary for complex math and science studies.

Computer simulations transform risky and expensive experiments into safe and cost-effective procedures. The Internet offers virtual reality settings where students can manipulate parameters, contexts, and scenarios. Computer simulations are a good example of the power of technology to improve the learning process. The flight simulator has been used for decades as the initial step in training airplane pilots. A flight simulator offers trainees the opportunity to practice the proper skills to control the plane and deal with emergency situations without risking lives or property loss. Although flight simulators can be complex and expensive machines, no pilot training program would question their utility. Simulators also are becoming essential tools in medical training. Through their use, medical students and residents are introduced to risky and invasive procedures without endangering patients' lives or exposing them to unnecessary pain and discomfort. Simulations are particularly helpful in situations that are too risky, expensive, or time-consuming to allow real-life experiments.

For instance, welding simulators have proved to be a cost-effective method to train future welders. Without simulators, this training requires long hours of practice and burning expensive electrodes. Simulations also enable students to test explosive materials virtually without running the risk of real explosions, and to experiment on animals without the ethical implications of real-life procedures. For elementary and secondary school students-and sometimes even for adults-exploring the

Internet can be a fun and enriching experience, or a frustrating adventure in trivia. Teachers and instructors play an important role as guides and facilitators by providing background material and guidelines for the search. They also need to monitor the process, particularly for younger students, who tend to browse the Web, rather than follow structured search plans. Teachers and instructors also are instrumental in helping students to separate unreliable sources from reliable ones and make sense of the large amount of information that may overwhelm them.

Globalization, creativity, and collaboration are key words in the modern workplace, where employers and employees are expected to share knowledge and work together toward common goals. In traditional classrooms, students work in isolation, doing tasks that emphasize conformism and boost competition. Trained in such environments, students may leave the school ill prepared to share ideas, divide tasks, or accept different points of view. Since ICTs can overcome physical and geographical barriers and facilitate communication, they have the potential to eliminate the artificial boundaries between schools and the outside world, and promote an environment that emphasizes collaboration rather than competition. Videos and computer animations enable students to "witness" a volcano eruption to learn about pressure, rock formation, or psychological and sociological responses to crises.

A simple radio or tape recorder can allow students in a foreign language class to listen to native speech regardless of their teachers' origin. Better yet, with interactive technologies, such as two-way radios or video-conferencing, students can communicate with native speakers without leaving their classrooms. Videos,

DVDs, computer software, and the Internet bring to schools anywhere in the world information that can be obtained only through the use of powerful scientific instruments that no single school can afford. More than any other technology, the Internet opens new opportunities for collaborative work. From group discussions to full collaborative research, the Internet has the potential to connect classrooms to research centers and students to actual scientists, as does the Global Learning and Observations to Benefit the Environment (GLOBE). Research on the Apple Classrooms of Tomorrow (ACOT) indicates that technology-rich classrooms promote teamwork and encourage tolerance for alternative viewpoints, two essential skills for increasingly complex and diverse workplaces.

Learning is only one component of the educational process, and quality learning cannot be attained without good teaching. Yet, teachers in general, and good teachers in particular, are in short supply even in developed countries. In the United States, for instance, the National Commission on Teaching and America's Future anticipates the need to hire an additional two million teachers in all teaching fields over the next decade to replace an increasingly aging work-force. For developing countries, in rural areas and in some specialties such as math and science, the teacher shortage has become critical. Simply hiring a teacher does not ensure quality education. To be effective, teachers must keep abreast of new perspectives on learning theories and their area of specialization, a task that becomes impossible when teachers work in distant, isolated areas. The mentoring process that has been used traditionally to prepare new cadres is an extra burden on experienced teachers, particularly in places where they are already in short supply.

Some schools of education are using videotaped sessions to prepare new teachers to enter the classroom without relying solely on mentors. The process frequently involves videotaping experienced teachers during regular classroom time. Student teachers observe their experienced peers in action, analyzing in detail the strategies used to present the material and interact with the students. The trainees then practice mock lessons with a group of peers or volunteer students while being videotaped. Peers and instructors review the tapes, highlighting weaknesses and strengths and making suggestions for improvement. Only after completing this process is the student teacher sent into actual classrooms.

Videos can also be used to analyze teaching styles and idiosyncrasies and help educational systems to change their approaches. A research related to the Third International Mathematics and Science Study (TIMSS) videotaped mathematics and science teachers in Japan, Germany, and the United States. The study analyzed variations in teaching style and lesson content among the three countries, looking for correlations between those dimensions and students' performance.

ICTs can be used as tools for training and support of teachers, regardless of their geographical dispersion. Scripted lessons in conjunction with educational programs via radio and television, such as the IRI and Telesecundaria, ensure that all students receive quality, updated information, while imparting to inexperienced and generalist teachers the appropriate content knowledge and new pedagogical strategies. The use of technology for teacher training has at least three major advantages: it reduces travel costs, avoids disrupting classroom routines, and familiarizes the teachers with the technology.

The Internet has myriad Websites to help teachers develop or improve lesson plans, exchange ideas, obtain information, and find free animations and simulations to enliven their lessons. Most Internet-based collaborative learning include teacher support and training, and conference proceedings are published regularly on the Web. Chat rooms or forums may become a laboratory for new ideas. For instance, teachers in Soweto, South Africa, used their online connection with schools in Birmingham, U.K., to create a support network and promote discussions on curriculum reform and school management practices. Indeed, contrary to the notion that technology is replacing the teacher, ICTs have expanded the quantity and quality of resources available to making teaching a less lonely endeavour.

More important still, research indicates that the introduction of ICTs for educational purposes has the potential to bring positive changes to teaching practices. In a survey of more than 2,000 teachers and school principals across the United States, the teachers stated that the technology helped them to become more effective (92% of respondents) and creative (88%). Both teachers and administrators agreed that technology had reinforced instruction, and functioned as a motivator for the students, who were more prone to ask questions and participate in the lessons.

Despite this potential for training and support, ICTs have not been accepted easily among teachers. Some complain that scripted lessons take away their ability to address students' individual differences and improve their own teaching strategies. Others fear that technologies will reduce the role of teachers in defining curriculum and educational strategies, or totally replace them.

Education policy development is an intricate process that requires reliable, timely, user-friendly data. ICTs can be valuable for storing and analyzing data on education indicators; student assessments; educational, physical, and human infrastructure; and cost and finance. The use of computer-related technology is particularly helpful in this field. For instance, administrators and policy makers can construct virtual scenarios around different policy options to determine needs and analyze potential consequences. Each scenario can be analyzed and evaluated systematically, not only in terms of its educational desirability, but also in terms of financial affordability, feasibility, and sustainability over a sufficient period of time to show results. The same elements of computing and telecommunications equipment and service that have made businesses more efficient and cost-effective can be applied to schools and educational systems.

ICTs can help administrators and school principals to streamline operations, monitor performance, and improve use of physical and human resources. More than other technologies, computer-related technologies have the potential to support the management of complex, standards-related instructional processes in relatively simple ways. They also can promote communication among schools, parents, central decision makers, and businesses, thus fostering accountability, public support, and connectivity with the marketplace. For instance, the Union City School District, located in one of the most impoverished communities in the United States, accepted an offer from the local telephone company to install computers in a pilot middle school and the homes of its teachers and parents. All those involved received training. The communication significantly among parents, teachers, and school administrators and was expanded to include other schools. An example of the use of computer-related technologies to address increasing demands in a time of reduced resources is provided by the Joint Board of Teacher Education (JBTE) in the Western Caribbean.

The effectiveness of ICTs-the realization of their potential-depends to a large extent on the context and quality of application. Moreover, since ICTs are only tools for education, it is difficult to isolate the factors that may be contributing to a positive result-such as educational philosophy, quality of teaching, parent support, and students' characteristics.

With these caveats in mind, evidence from large studies and meta-analyses suggests that use of ICTs, particularly computer technologies, is correlated to positive academic outcomes, including higher test scores, better attitudes toward schools, and better understanding of abstract concepts. A longitudinal study of a statewide experiment with computers in the classroom found that those most in need of help-low-income, low-achieving students, and students with disabilities-made the most gains.

ICT for Education : Prerequisites and Constraints

This section focuses on prerequisites and constraints that influence the use of information and communication technologies as tools to expand and improve education, with an emphasis on current status and existing trends and on possible ways to overcome identified barriers. To facilitate the analysis, the factors identified are organized schematically into three broad areas: access, acceptance, and availability.

1. *Access*—includes the basic requisites for the installation and use of technologies:

   — Infrastructure-foundations for the technology

   — Costs and finance mechanisms

   — Legal frameworks-laws and regulations that facilitate or constrain the use of technologies for the proposed objectives.

2. *Acceptance*—cultural and political factors that create or promote barriers to technology:

   — Cultural perspectives-nationalism, traditions, attitude toward innovations

   — Political perspectives-priorities, interests, and negotiation power

   — Interest groups-influence of unions, businesses, parents, and other groups

   — Educational systems-objective, structure, and organization.

3. *Availability*—technology-related factors that facilitate or hinder implementation:

   — Contentware—what the technology can offer in terms of content, language, quality, and relevance of material

   — Experts—presence or absence of qualified staff who can implement a quality programmes.

   — Capacity building-interest in building or ability to build an expert workforce.

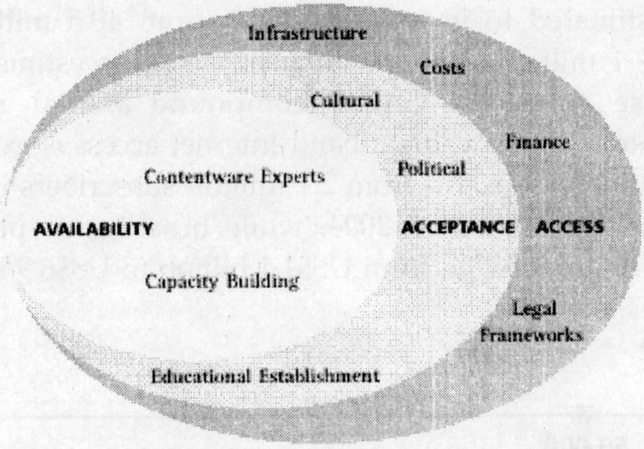

Figure 1: Prequeisited Constraints ion the use of the technology for education

Five major trends have characterized the development of ICTs:

— *Complementarity*—ICTs complement, rather than replace each other. Videoconferencing and digital radio are two examples of how different technologies are associated to improve results.

— *Speed of growth*—ICTs have grown exponentially. In 1950, personal computers were little known or used, but within a generation, they became essential work and communication tools. The number of Internet hosts worldwide grew more than 1,100 times in eight years Figure 2. Reduced costs-Increased use of ICTs is associated with reduced costs and improved technology. This trend is particularly felt in the computer industry, where hardware prices have fallen, despite significant increases in memory and speed. Internet access is another area where growth has been accompanied by some cost reduction. From 1999 to 2004, the number of U.S. households online is estimated to increase by 66% (from 40.5 million to 67.1 million), but spending on access is estimated to rise only 9.2% CAGR (compound annual growth rate). Similarly, broadband Internet access is expected to increase 800%, from 2.1 million subscribers in 1999 to 18.9 million in 2004, while broadband spending will grow 527%, from US$1.1 billion to US$6.9 billion, respectively.

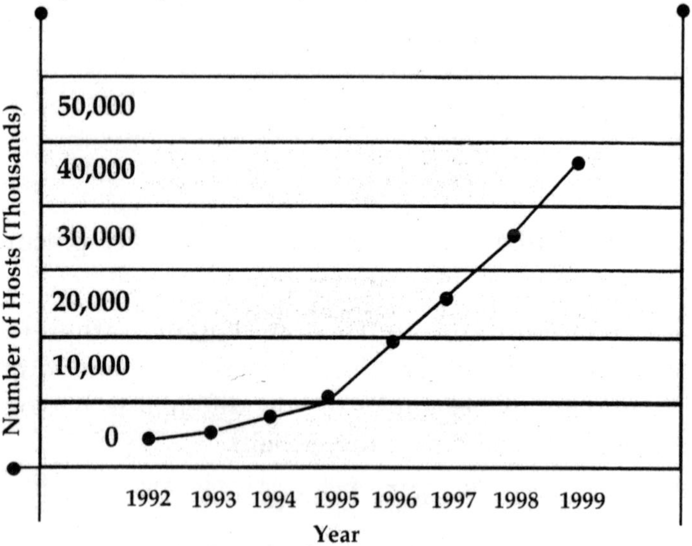

Figure 2: Growth of internet hosts worldwide

— *Simplification*—ICTs strive for simplicity of use, even when the technology becomes gradually more complex. The first disk operating system- (DOS-) operated personal computers (PCs) required some training for simple tasks; however, children have no problems dealing with modern PCs. This concern with the user may explain, at least partially, the rapid popularity of the medium.

— *Problem-solving focus*—Perhaps more than any other technology, ICTs strive for efficiency: they are faster, simpler, less costly, and more productive. This search for efficiency propels ICTs to continuous improvements. Auto industries have relied on one source of fuel for the past 100 years, despite warnings ranging from potential extinction of this sole source to environmental disasters. In less than 50 years, telecommunications have experimented with simple telephone lines, fiber optic cables, satellites, and wireless technologies, and research continues. These characteristics encourage and challenge a planning process that aims at introducing technology in education. The encouragement comes from the fact that educational agencies and countries can leapfrog from pretechnology stages (e.g., the absence of telephone lines) to state-of-the-art strategy (e.g., wireless technologies), thus bypassing less efficient and generally more expensive alternatives. The challenge is that technology planners must be creative and look toward the future to ensure they are not missing a better and less costly option.

— *Access to ICTs and the digital divide*—Access to modern information and communication technologies varies greatly around the world. Until now, ICTs have not corrected the divide between technology-rich and technology-poor countries initiated with the Industrial Revolution. In the United States, for instance, there is a correlation between race and computer ownership or Internet access. Whites are more likely to own a computer than blacks, even when controlling for differences in education, except for those at the highest income levels. Between December 1998 and August 2000, the gap in Internet access between black households and the national average grew from 15% to 18%; for Latino households, the gap grew from 14% to 18%. In China, significant differences exist in age and gender among Internet users-approximately 50% of Internet users are between 18 and 24 years of age and 75% are male. A similar trend is found in Brazil, where 61% of the Internet users are male, and 56% are aged 14-24. Access to ICTs depends on three basic prerequisites: infrastructure, costs and financing mechanisms, and legal frameworks.

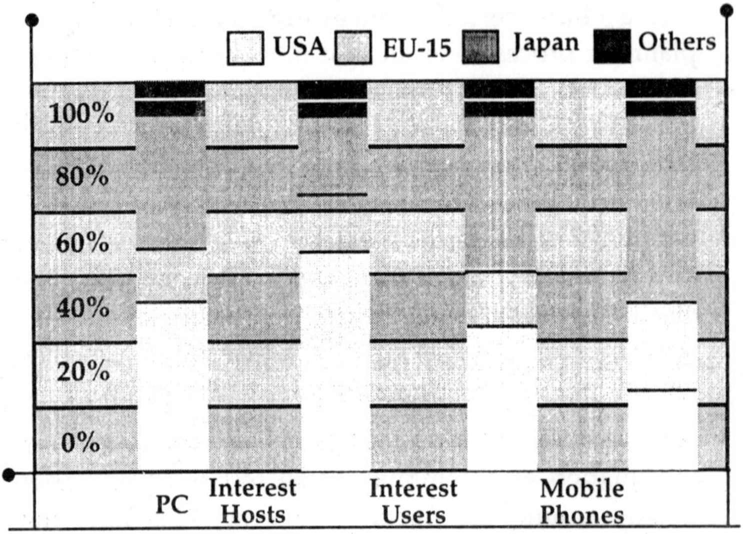

Figure 3: The Information society (per 100 inhabitants)

Until recently, most information and communication technologies depended on electric power and telephone lines. The production and consumption of energy varies broadly across countries in direct relationship with their economic development. Developing countries tend to have lower levels of energy production, less efficient systems that produce great loses during transmission and distribution, and lower consumption levels. On average, poor countries consume 5% of the energy consumed by wealthy countries. The consumption range is wide, varying from 21KWh in Ethiopia to approximately 24,000 KWh in Norway.

Availability of telephone mainlines follows similar distribution: wealthier countries-and wealthier regions within a country-have more phone lines per inhabitant than countries and regions with weaker economies. In South Asia, urban residents will be five times more likely to have telephone lines, in contrast with the European Union, where the ratio between urban and nonurban areas is approximately 1:1. Within the same world region, differences also can be significant. In Latin America and the Caribbean, for instance, Chile has 203 mainlines per 1,000 (281 in the largest city), while Haiti has eight (17 in the cities). In the Middle East, the United Arab Emirates have 389 mainlines per 1,000 (374 in the largest city), while Iraq has 31 and 75, respectively.

Costs strongly influence access. Despite reduction in costs in the past decades, indicators still show significant cost differences among countries and within countries in a single region. In 1999, average monthly rates for Internet access in Latin America ranged from US$81.71 in Trinidad & Tobago to US$12.75 in Peru, with a regional average at US$36.23. Business's rates are much higher. In Bermuda, for instance, businesses can pay more than US$850 a month for unlimited Internet access.

As a means of mass communication, radio has many advantages: it has broad outreach, is relatively inexpensive, is easy to use, and is present in almost all households around the world. In addition, radio programs are less expensive to produce than television, videos, or computer software. Although radio lacks the visual effects of television and computers, educational programs broadcast via radio have popular appeal. Most of all, radio does not require complex infrastructures. Battery, windup, or solar-powered radios ensure transmission even where electricity is not available or dependable. Walker describes a portable FM radio system operated entirely by solar power, part of the Commonwealth of Learning Media Empowerment (COLME) in Uganda.

To overcome the limited and unreliable electricity supply in the region, staff built a structure with eight solar panels and seven deep cycle batteries. This structure provides all the lighting and power needed to operate the station during the 18-hour broadcast day. In addition, the solar installations have a life span of more than 10 years and low maintenance costs.

If a 'catch-up' strategy seems doomed to fail, the technological search for faster, broader, and more efficient means of communication offers new hope to countries or regions with limited infrastructures. Trends in ICTs include:

— *Digital radio*—The association of streaming technology and the conversion from analog to digital radio broadcasting enabled radio stations to reach global audiences. Different from analog radio, where the power of transmitters is essential for broadcasting success, digital radio has low power requirements, which means lower operating costs. This capability enables smaller stations to offer power and quality similar to their wealthier competitors. In addition, digital audio broadcasting allows for transmission of text or graphic information that can be displayed on a small screen on a digital radio. This increases the usefulness of radio as an educational tool, particularly for disciplines where visualization is an essential decoder, such as foreign language, mathematics, or science.

— *Satellites*—Satellites have been used to transmit multimedia information, including television broadcast, for many decades. The large, geostationary satellites orbit Earth at high altitudes (36,000 Km), and data are sent to the satellites and back to large terrestrial transceivers through high-frequency beams. The technology is expensive and limited in quality, with a long propagation delay-about 0.25 sec.-which restricts its use for voice transmission. More recently, low earth-orbiting satellites (LEOs) are being launched. These are small, computerized devices that circle Earth at high speeds and low altitudes (780 Km). Their short propagation delay-about 12 msec. and virtually error-free connections to ground stations make them popular tools for wireless communication. In addition, LEOs' receivers can be very small, thus increasing their outreach mobility. To compensate for the expensive technology, particularly in the case of geostationary satellites, regional partnerships are multiplying. The Regional African Satellite Communications (RASCOM) is an organization of 44 African nations that aim at connecting all major African cities via satellite network. RedHUCyT is a satellite-based network of higher education and research institutions in the United States and Latin America, with support from the Organization of American States.

Cables, wireless, and others—As communication moves from e-mail to complex electronic transactions, capacity or bandwidth requirements increase. Traditional telephone lines are no longer sufficient to carry the amount and type of information that is being exchanged electronically. A simple 2400-baud connection can only transmit about 240 characters per second of an e-mail message. Audio and video applications through the Internet require a minimum of 14.4Kbps, and videoconferencing needs 128Kbps.

The expansion of the Internet and, more recently, e-commerce created a new demand for more bandwidth. The bandwidth demand between Europe and the United States is expected to grow by approximately 80% a year. In response, digital subscriber line (DSL) cable and alternative proposals are multiplying, mostly through private companies' efforts to ensure their share of a promising e-market. Between 1995 and 1997, the private circuit capacity between the United States and other OECD (Organisation for Economic Co-operation and Development) countries had a compound increase of 172% and surpassed the capacity allocated to international message services.

Education factors may profit from this market-driven growth. In the past 10 years, wireless technologies have gained increasing acceptance among residential and business users. However, they should not be seen as the solution for all the problems with infrastructure. Start-up costs are high, and requires highly trained technicians; some wavebands are highly sensitive to weather conditions, thus increasing the probability of errors, and they require a high level of coordination to avoid interfering with other radio spectrum users. In places with an already well-developed network, fiber optic cables offer more transmission capacity with smaller margins of errors and at lower cost. Where the infrastructure is missing, wireless technologies may be a solution, even if only a temporary one.

Considering the speed of change in the ICTs industry, discussions on the use of ICTs for educational purposes should focus not only on the technologies available, but also on those that are in the planning stage, and should evaluate how feasible and affordable they are for each specific case.

As stated earlier, decisions on the use of technology for education are, first of all, educational decisions. Yet, the immediate costs of a technology have greater impact on decision makers than its potential benefits. Discussions on costs of the educational uses of technology tend to compare traditional and technology-mediated approaches as if they had similar purposes. For instance, estimates of higher education costs compare campus universities with distance learning as if they served the same group of students. Similarly, research on the use of technology for elementary and secondary students uses traditional measures of outcomes, such as standardized test scores, to compare technology conventional approaches. Results may be disappointing, with many studies concluding that the two approaches have similar results, but the technology-assisted approach is more costly.

Missing in those studies is an approach whereby technology for education is not viewed as a replacement for face-to-face methodologies, but, rather, to attain objectives that have not been attained efficiently otherwise: expanding access, promoting equality, improving the internal efficiency of educational systems, enhancing the quality of education, and preparing new and old generations for a technology-driven marketplace. For each of these objectives, different technologies may prove more or less cost-effective depending on two aspects:

The characteristics of the technologies: Producing a television program, for example, is 10 times more expensive than producing a radio program. While radio may reach a broader audience, television has a visual impact that is missing in radio. Computer-related technologies are costlier than radio or television, but they have greater potential to promote higher-order thinking skills activities while familiarizing students with a technology that is becoming essential in the workplace.

Specific conditions where the technologies will be used: These include local infrastructures, availability of expertise, and appropriate contentware, as well as regulatory and cultural obstacles.

Educational factors frequently suffer from having only short-term objectives. Within this perspective, investing in technology may not seem reasonable. However, research shows that Interactive Radio Instruction (IRI) and television factors (such as Telesecundaria) can increase retention rates and improve academic performance. Likewise, appropriate use of computers in schools has been shown to improve academic outcomes.

By reducing the number of years a student spends in the system and producing better-prepared workers, technology-mediated, improve the efficiency and effectiveness of educational systems and promote savings in the long run. Cost comparisons based solely on short-term objectives will not reflect those savings.

Curran proposes a simple formula to estimate costs in technology factors: TC = FC+VC(N), where:

— TC (Total cost) is the sum of fixed costs plus the product of variable costs multiplied by the output, N;

— N is the output, generally measured as number of students served, number of graduates, or student. contact hours;

— FC (Fixed costs) are the costs incurred with the development and initial implementation of the include new buildings, or renovation of old ones, buying and installing hardware, and all expenses related to the development and production of courses, programs, and related material; and

— VC (variable costs), sometimes called recurrent costs, include expenses related to administration of the programme, training, distribution of material and supplies, and student support.

The problem is not so simple. Administrative cost (a variable cost) does not change linearly with variations in the number of students served (N). These costs will remain constant until N increases, or is reduced by 10%, after which, the administration will have to be adjusted, although by smaller proportions. He calculates that a 20% increase in the numbers of student increases administration costs by 7%.

Understanding this balance between fixed and variable costs is key to technology-mediated factors. As a rule of thumb, it can be said that:

— Technology-mediated with high fixed costs and low variable costs, such as those involving radio and television, have greater potential for economies of scale.

— Technologies that replace conventional teaching, rather than complement it, also have an immediate cost advantage, since personnel tends to be the largest component of the variable costs in education.

— Technologies with high variable costs and that work in conjunction with conventional teaching are unlikely to bring short-term cost advantages; in the long run, though, they may reduce costs by increasing the · quality and efficiency of the system.

For a lower-income country, the scale of the programmes is a key variable. A small-scale programmes (100,000 students) may represent as much as 84% of the potential discretionary public spending on primary education for the country, while a large-scale (1 million students) represents only 23%. For upper-middle-income countries, the relationship between scale of the potential discretionary spending is less significant: 7% for a small-scale programmes and 2% for a large-scale one.

For computer, infrastructure preparation and hardware are the largest part of the bill, but savings can be obtained if schools act in coordination. A school district has greater purchasing power to negotiate volume discounts than each school has separately. For instance, the U.S. state of North Carolina buys telecommunications equipment and services for all of its schools, saving up to 50% on some items. Partnering also allows schools to share resources, including software, Internet connections, training programs, and full-time support staff, thus reducing significantly the overall cost of the programmes.

Legal frameworks

In planning a technology-mediated programmes for education, attention must be paid to the laws and regulations that will affect the programmes, either facilitate it or create barriers to it. ICTs, with their ability to reach beyond political boundaries, defy many of the national and international legal frameworks that were created for a world with frontiers. Solutions, albeit necessary, are difficult to find and slow to implement. Proposals that have been advanced by experts include the following.

Telecommunication monopolies and restrictive regulations have been part of strategic defense programs in many countries; however, calls for deregulation and liberalization of this sector are now heard everywhere. Deregulation is expected to bring competition, thus promoting more supplies and lower prices. While protecting equal access to all must remain a central concern, there is evidence that government-controlled monopolies are not always the best answer in a fast-moving technological environment. In Europe, leased-line capacity expanded significantly in countries that liberalized their telecommunication frameworks. In Denmark, Finland, and Norway, for example, the direct leased-line capacity with the United States in 1995 was seven times that of Sweden. Sweden moved toward deregulation, and, two years later, its leased-line capacity was 11 times greater than the three countries' combined total. In many countries, local education authorities are profiting from liberalization of telecommunication services by entering into agreements with private providers, many of which see agreements with community-based programmes as a public relations investment that enhances the company's image and increases its local support.

Accreditation and certification must in the long run maintain confidence in educational offerings by guaranteeing their quality and the acquisition of qualifications both to individuals and to employers. Systems of accreditation developed for concrete institutions may not apply in the virtual environment. Regulations on building safety or student/ instructor ratios do not pertain to the virtual world. Credit hour is another concept that does not fit distance learning. Created to protect students in the traditional learning environment, accreditations might become a barrier against a global education market.

A student may be discouraged from taking online courses if the institution offering them is not accredited in his or her country, regardless of how prestigious the institution may be. Countries with centralized education may have an advantage in terms of recognizing credentials or facilitating transfer of credits. Decentralization, in this case, may be one more obstacle for students and institutions alike. Country, state, and local regulations can be mutually exclusive, making it cumbersome or potentially impossible to create distance-learning programmes that meet the diverse requirements. The members of the European Union began conversations on ways to simplify regulations and recognize qualifications and credentials across country borders, but such discussions are still rare.

Intellectual Property

Since 1886, with the Berne Convention, and later with the Universal Copyright Convention-administered by UNESCO-as revised at Paris on July 1971, countries have recognized the rights of an author over his or her intellectual property. Laws also have been enacted to ensure the financial remuneration of authors and protect the integrity of their work. Each new technology brings challenges to the existing laws, however. While users come to the Internet in search of more and free information, producers look for ways to expand copyright laws and ensure their rights. The Trade-Related Intellectual Property Rights (TRIPS), negotiated under the World Trade Organization (WTO) umbrella, establishes new arrangements for technology-related intellectual property that cover software code. Developing countries see TRIPS as a tool to give developed countries control over the benefits of the new economy. Developed countries, on the other hand, argue that strong intellectual property laws are necessary to promote economic growth and development that eventually will benefit all. For educators, these laws may appear cumbersome. Kerrey and Isakson cite the case of a music instructor who can use songs and pieces of music in her classroom, but has to draft numerous letters seeking permission from copyright holders to incorporate these works into an online version of the same class. Yet, educators and researchers are also rightly interested in preserving their property rights. These global discussions bring to the table problems of jurisdiction and the anachronism of legal systems developed for societies enclosed within political boundaries. The balance among national and global interests, rights of individuals, and freedom of information is a challenge that must be faced if the potential of ICTs is to be fulfilled. International organizations, such as UNESCO, can have a leadership role in bringing stakeholders together to face this challenge.

Ensuring access to technologies is just one step in the success of ICT-mediated educational programmes. Cultural and political factors may promote or create obstacles to the use of technology or limit its use to certain subgroups of society. Likewise, the structure and organization of local educational systems may favour integration of technology or create a technophobe atmosphere that hinders efforts to change. Overall, acceptance of technologies has not been a problem.

ICTs have been well received worldwide, and it appears that the older technologies opened the door for the more recent ones. In India, places that did not have a telephone now have Internet kiosks where families can e-mail their relatives abroad.

Radio and television are now part of the world culture. However, computer and Internet use is still dominated and controlled by a small group of predominantly wealthy, educated, urban males. Regardless of the country, the data are very similar. For instance, males constitute 61% of the Internet users in Europe, 71% in Argentina, and 67% in Korea.

Students and professionals make up 70% of Internet users in Russia and in China, 86% of whom have college degrees. Access is a key issue, but access alone does not explain the data. The elderly and women, even in urban areas, trail behind young and men in ICT use. Surveys on acceptance of computer-related technologies among these population subgroups were not found; yet, anecdotal information from the field suggests that males and females of all ages and cultural backgrounds are potentially open to technologies that improve their lives and put them in contact with the world.

The Telecenters or the Virtual Souks (markets), prove that rural populations are open to technologies that connect them with the world and improve their standard of living. The challenge to expanding ICTs to rural populations is more political than technological. Government employees and businesses tend to see rural areas as bad investments. Still, experiments with carefully planned rural programmes have been successful and even profitable.

The Village Phone program of the Grameen Bank in Bangladesh installs rural telephones in strategic points that can be accessed by hundreds of local villagers. Women staff the programmes to facilitate access by both men and women. One telecommunication operator say that 1,500 rural "public calling offices" generate as much revenue as 12,000 urban subscribers to cellular telephones. Likewise, by charging users' fees, telecenters in rural areas of Africa are becoming self-sustaining and are, in fact, expanding.

With few exceptions, generally related to religious beliefs, cultural factors seem to have little effect on the acceptance of technology. But, attention to cultural differences when implementing technological innovation is essential to avoid unintended consequences. Internet use among the elderly is growing. From 1999 to 2000, Internet use among North American women aged 55 and over grew by 110%, making it the subgroup with the second-largest growth in the country, just behind teenage girls. Educating the elderly is a measure of good economic and social policies. The median age of the world's population is rising, and among the elderly, the older subgroup is the fastest-growing group. Medical knowledge indicates that an active life is the best protection against emotional and physical illnesses, regardless of age. Moreover, in some countries, such as those devastated by the AIDS epidemic, the elderly already are assuming the unexpected roles of principal breadwinners and caretakers of orphaned children.

Preparing them for these responsibilities is essential to reduce the emotional and economic impact of changed roles. These are the strategies required to learn new technologies. China is catering to its elderly population through the Universities of the Third Age (UTA). UTAs use distance learning technologies—from postal correspondence to the Internet—to reach urban and rural elderly across the country. The rapid growth of the UTAs reflects not only the large demand, but also the ability of the elderly to adjust to alternative learning environments mediated through technology.

In many developing countries, women are caught in a circle of poverty, illiteracy, and cultural traditions that function as barriers to computer-related technologies, which are expensive, literacy dependent, and defined as a male realm. The stereotypical view of computers as male tools exists even in developed countries. Research in the United States shows that girls are not expected to excel in technology and are given less encouragement to use computers or pursue a career in the field. Parents buy computer-related gifts for boys more often than for girls, and teachers in technology classes tend to give more time and assistance to boys than girls. The fact that training generally is provided by men adds one more barrier, particularly in countries that impose limits on contact between genders. The scarcity of female role models in technology-related professions is another disincentive on a path already full of obstacles. Yet, research shows that, when girls are given the same opportunities and support provided to boys.

Since the reasons for the problem are varied, the solutions must be multiple. Suggestions include:

— At the elementary and secondary school level-train teachers and school administrators to understand their biases in relation to girls and technology and develop strategies to overcome this bias; train female teachers as technology instructors; work with parents to encourage or support their daughters' interest in technology; encourage and support girls to participate in computer clubs and other technology-related activities.

— At the tertiary level-implement public and/or private scholarships targeted to women pursuing technology careers, and provide encouragement and support for those who are in predominantly male schools, including offering opportunities for studies abroad.

— For adult education-include female instructors in telecenters to ease women's transition into technology; educate the public to understand that technology promotes economic growth for the whole family; promote programmes targeting women, since men can profit from them as well, while the reverse may not happen.

Acceptance of technology is also related to the level of political support or resistance at local and national levels. National governments have been key players in the expansion of educational programmes that depend on technology. Most mega-universities have privileged access to telecommunication systems that is controlled or regulated by the government in their base country. Countries such as Brazil and China have invested massively in infrastructures and financed educational programmes to spread computers into the schools. Mexico's Telesecundaria is a federally funded programme, and many IRI and telecenter programmes include partnerships between governments and international funding agencies. In 1994, Botswana developed a national strategy for the use of computer technology in secondary education and integrated a

Computer Awareness Program for the Junior Community Secondary Schools in its Nine-Year Basic Education Program. The South Korean government is promoting a nationwide strategy that uses computer technology to foster an open and lifelong learning society. Measures that government can take to support and expand technology-mediated programmes include:

— Invest in infrastructures.

— Review fiscal policy to favour educational and nonprofit use of technologies.

— Deregulate telecommunication monopolies while protecting educational use of telecommunications.

— Reorient funding policies to serve students, rather than institutions.

— Fund technology-mediated programmes directly or encourage these programmes through tax relief and other benefits.

— Access to technology for underrepresented populations.

— Promote teacher training that uses technology to familiarize teachers with these tools.

— Simplify regulations and accreditation requirements to facilitate transfer of credits across states or neighbouring countries.

— Implement standards of quality for distance education courses.

— Foster progressive policies on education that encourage activities related to higher-order thinking skills rather than memorization.

Interest groups outside the educational establishment may have powerful influence on promoting or creating obstacles to the use of technology for education. Digital corporations, such as Apple, funded pioneer computer experiments in schools. Many technology giants, such as Lucent Technologies, are directly involved in providing training. Policies to attracting more such groups to educational programmes at the elementary and secondary levels is a way to expand the support base for the programme, ensure expertise, and improve the programme's effectiveness.

Within the education establishment, acceptance of technologies is an issue, and the expansion of distance learning institutions has been met with its share of resistance. Teachers, from basic to higher education, are essential to the success or failure of educational programmes, but rarely are they involved in the planning stage of these programmes. Despite all the rhetoric about modernization, teacher education programs rarely include technology as content or strategy. Graduates of most teacher training institutions have little experience in using technology and no information about how to integrate ICTs into curricula and practice.

The technology is mostly seen as an add-on to traditional classroom teaching, and many times as an unfamiliar, and therefore, threatening imposition. An add-on approach inhibits the potential of the technology to improve the quality and effectiveness of education and decreases support from parents, students, and the public in general, who see technology as an expensive investment with no visible trade-off. Totally integrating use of technology into the teaching/learning process presents another challenge. Teachers may feel they are losing control over the content of the course and the students. The path from center of instruction to facilitator requires a new paradigm, and many teachers are not prepared to make the change.

Distance learning stretches the paradigm even further. The personal interaction that had been the basis of the teacher-learner society is no longer there. For students, the distance learning approach may be seen as depriving them from contact with the teacher-although many times, this contact in a campus university is a myth as a weekly class for 300 or more students jams into an auditorium. For instructors, distance education requires greater preparation for planning and production, extra training in technology, and less control over students' reactions to the material. It also brings concerns over job security.

For schools and universities, distance education requires greater investment, including preparation and delivery of materials ahead of class time, ensuring office hours for student queries related to academic content and to technology issues, access to library and other resources, and an efficient system of tutoring and support. Yet, changes in the student population and their interests, employee demand for training and retraining of the workforce, and market pressures will be the determining forces in the expansion of technology-mediated learning.

The movement toward distance education has the potential to bring cultural changes that have yet to be understood fully. The use of imported standardized packages will impose extraneous cultural values on developing nations. The result of a movement toward a learner-centered, more specialized education may be a fragmented education that will preclude the "civilizing function" that has historically been associated with universities. In other words, the boundary-less characteristic of distance education seems to equally threaten the existence of national cultures and of a universal culture shared by all educated human beings. These are epistemological concerns that raise a new perspective on the social role of education in the years to come. Few studies on cultural and political influences over the acceptance or rejection of technology-mediated educational details are available. More is known about teachers' reaction toward technology. In general, this reaction moves from resistance to acceptance as soon as the value of technology is understood. Ensuring access to the technology without promoting its acceptance may lead to an under used programme. Likewise, securing access and acceptance without availability of content, experts, and a potential for capacity building may result in a well-received but short-lived programme plagued by technological glitches.

Educational materials for ICTs are easy to find; the challenge is to find good materials that incorporate sound pedagogical strategies and use the potential of the adopted technology fully. Two basic criteria that must be taken into account when evaluating an education material are quality and viability. The quality of a product can be judged through direct examination, references, reviews, testimonials from users, or awards. Viability is related to the useful life of the product. A good product that maintains its usefulness for a long period will produce reasonable returns on the investment. This is easier when the potential number of users is large, posing particular challenges for groups limited in size by language, culture, or educational needs. Many organizations have developed criteria to evaluate contentware, particularly software, but each educational system should define its own standards to reflect the programmes objectives and curricular requirements and the specific needs of students and teachers. The use of commercially developed material saves time and avoids production costs, but also has disadvantages, such as:

— The material may not meet local curriculum standards or educational objectives;

— The content will reflect the ideologies and lifestyles of the producing country, generally the United States;

— For non-English-speaking countries, language is a barrier; and

— Most of all, product licensing and royalties can erase the savings realized at the production stage.

Sharing materials among countries is a better option when agreements on royalties can be reached. Sharing is easier for countries with the same language and similar customs, and for topics that have a more universal nature, such as mathematics and science. Translations, albeit expensive, may prove cost-effective, and software translators are becoming common, although the quality of their work is still questionable. Partnerships with universities, broadcasting, or software companies offer another prospect for obtaining educational materials that are customized to a country's reality and needs.

Open-source software is a response from the digital community to the increased control of technology-related property by large corporations. Not all open-source programmes are free, although most require only nominal fees or voluntary contributions.

The movement regulates itself through ethical norms that ensure recognition to the author and protect the integrity of the product, while encouraging new product development. Since the program codes are open to reviews and improvements from a number of experts, the quality of open-source software tends to be superior to that of commercial products. In addition, the programs can be customized to the user's specific needs. One disadvantage is that most programs are written for UNIX or Linux, two platforms that require technical expertise to use. For developing countries, the open-source movement makes it easier to obtain high-quality products, avoid the costs of commercial software, and develop an expert workforce. Rather than buying a package of commercial software for each of its computers, a school district in a developed country can hire a skilled programmer to configure an open-source material to the district's specific needs and duplicate it for as many computers as necessary. The district will have a quality product for less cost, without infringing on national or international laws. In addition, the process stimulates growth of local programmers, supported by an international network of experts.

In technology-mediated programmes, two different types of expertise are required: the technical expertise related to the hardware employed, and the content expertise in using the technology for educational purposes. Programmes fail when planners invest heavily in hardware and software, but minimally in hiring and training competent people, thus leaving the programme without expert support and guidance.

Equipment failures are common, particularly in the initial stages of programmes, when the lack of familiarity with the technology increases the numbers of errors. The more complex the equipment is, the greater the probability that technical problems will occur.

Continuous glitches will hamper the flow of information, reduce students' enthusiasm and motivation, and threaten the success of the programme. A teacher with a good working knowledge of the technology may be able to solve the most common problems. However, not all teachers are technology-savvy, nor are all technology problems easily solved. Rarely does an educational system have the luxury to pay for a technician to support the instructors and ensure that the hardware is functioning appropriately.

Technicians are difficult to find, and with the expansion of the digital industry, they are in great demand. Individuals with expertise in technology are finding jobs before graduation and offered salaries that educational systems can hardly afford. Training for educators generally is limited to use of specific programs or software packages; beyond that, educators are on their own. No institution will train educators to be technology experts, and few will provide them with a broad understanding of the requirements and potential of the technologies they will be using. Improvisation is currently the norm in this field. However, countries should look more carefully at technology for education.

The development of specialists in educational material reduces dependency on imported products, while increasing the probability that the language and content of the products are appropriate for the users. It also creates a workforce that brings a fresh perspective to a field controlled by a small group of producers-a competitive advantage in the global market of educational services. Over time, investments in this workforce will bring large returns. Education services constitute the fifth largest service export in the United States. In 1997 alone, the United States spent US$26 billion on education-related goods and services, including textbooks and supplementary materials (US$11.6 billion), technology (US$4.8 billion), and testing/test preparation (US$3 billion). The growth of educational expenditures is not limited to the United States. Worldwide sales of educational software to schools in 2000 were estimated to be US$4.1 billion, with another US$2.1 billion sold to consumer markets outside schools. By 2009, the education market is programmes to grow to US$200 million in India, US$580 million in South Africa, and US$1.7 billion in China.

Capturing this market is a tempting possibility for many commercial enterprises, particularly if developing countries choose to remain buyers rather than producers. Currently, few tertiary institutions and programmes seek to create this cadre of specialists. The Universidade de los Andes, in Colombia, has a programme focusing on the development of interactive games for education. The International Virtual Education Network (IVEN) for the Enhancement of Science and Mathematics Education in Latin America is forming teams of content experts, graphic designers, instructional designers, and programmers to develop educational material focused on mathematics and science for secondary eduction. A few universities in Latin America offer courses to train distance learning educators, such as the Universidade de Brasilia or the Universidad Abierta de Venezuela. This is a new frontier that merits careful attention and support from educators and decision makers.

In estimating an educational programmes's potential for success, decision makers should take into account four characteristics: desirability, feasibility, affordability, and sustainability. A desirable programme responds to identifiable needs and is more likely to garner support and funding. A feasible programme is one that may be accomplished within an established time frame, available personnel, and budget. Programmes that are badly planned and underfunded are less likely to fulfill their obligations within the proposed time. They also risk being discarded as failures, when, in truth, they were not given an opportunity to succeed.

Affordable is not synonymous with inexpensive. The concept of affordability is relative to the benefits expected from the programme in relation to its costs. Even if a large-scale IRI programme represents a high proportion of the potential discretionary public spending for primary education in lower-income countries, if it also reaches a substantial proportion of the country's young people who otherwise would be without schooling, it will surely be affordable over time. A programmes affordability must be estimated in comparison with the costs of building and maintaining traditional schools for all those children or maintaining the status quo.

Many parents and community members are willing to help a programme they consider helpful and one that gives them a feeling of ownership. Private enterprises may look at such programmes as a way to gain the support of potential clients. Successful programmes are careful to involve community members from the beginning.

Resolution Adopted by the General Assembly (without reference to Main Committee [A/55/L.2]) United Nations Millennium Declaration

The General Assembly Adopts the following Declaration:

United Nations Millennium Declaration

I. Values and principles

1. We, heads of State and Government, have gathered at United Nations Headquarters in New York from 6 to 8 September 2000, at the dawn of a new millennium, to reaffirm our faith in the Organization and its Charter as indispensable foundations of a more peaceful, prosperous and just world.

2. We recognize that, in addition to our separate responsibilities to our individual societies, we have a collective responsibility to uphold the principles of human dignity, equality and equity at the global level. As leaders we have a duty therefore to all the world's people, especially the most vulnerable and, in

particular, the children of the world, to whom the future belongs.

3. We reaffirm our commitment to the purposes and principles of the Charter of the United Nations, which have proved timeless and universal. Indeed, their relevance and capacity to inspire have increased, as nations and peoples have become increasingly interconnected and interdependent.

4. We are determined to establish a just and lasting peace all over the world in accordance with the purposes and principles of the Charter. We rededicate ourselves to support all efforts to uphold the sovereign equality of all States, respect for their territorial integrity and political independence, resolution of disputes by peaceful means and in conformity with the principles of justice and international law, the right to self-determination of peoples which remain under colonial domination and foreign occupation, non-interference in the internal affairs of States, respect for human rights and fundamental freedoms, respect for the equal rights of all without distinction as to race, sex, language or religion and international cooperation in solving international problems of an economic, social, cultural or humanitarian character.

5. We believe that the central challenge we face today is to ensure that globalization becomes a positive force for all the world's people. For while globalization offers great opportunities, at present its benefits are very unevenly shared, while its costs are unevenly distributed. We recognize that developing countries and countries with economies in transition face special difficulties in responding to this central

challenge. Thus, only through broad and sustained efforts to create a shared future, based upon our common humanity in all its diversity, can globalization be made fully inclusive and equitable. These efforts must include policies and measures, at the global level, which correspond to the needs of developing countries and economies in transition and are formulated and implemented with their effective participation.

6. We consider certain fundamental values to be essential to international relations in the twenty-first century. These include:

— *Freedom*: Men and women have the right to live their lives and raise their children in dignity, free from hunger and from the fear of violence, oppression or injustice. Democratic and participatory governance based on the will of the people best assures these rights.

— *Equality*: No individual and no nation must be denied the opportunity to benefit from development. The equal rights and opportunities of women and men must be assured.

— *Solidarity*: Global challenges must be managed in a way that distributes the costs and burdens fairly in accordance with basic principles of equity and social justice. Those who suffer or who benefit least deserve help from those who benefit most.

— *Tolerance*: Human beings must respect one other, in all their diversity of belief, culture and language. Differences within and between societies should be neither feared nor repressed, but cherished as a precious asset of humanity. A culture of peace and dialogue among all civilizations should be actively promoted.

— *Respect for nature*: Prudence must be shown in the management of all living species and natural resources, in accordance with the precepts of sustainable development. Only in this way can the immeasurable riches provided to us by nature be preserved and passed on to our descendants. The current unsustainable patterns of production and consumption must be changed in the interest of our future welfare and that of our descendants.

— *Shared responsibility*: Responsibility for managing worldwide economic and social development, as well as threats to international peace and security, must be shared among the nations of the world and should be exercised multilaterally. As the most universal and most representative organization in the world, the United Nations must play the central role.

7. In order to translate these shared values into actions, we have identified key objectives to which we assign special significance.

II. Peace, security and disarmament

8. We will spare no effort to free our peoples from the scourge of war, whether within or between States, which has claimed more than 5 million lives in the past decade. We will also seek to eliminate the dangers posed by weapons of mass destruction.

9. We resolve therefore:

— To strengthen respect for the rule of law in international as in national affairs and, in particular, to ensure compliance by Member States with the decisions of the International Court of Justice, in compliance with the Charter of the United Nations, in cases to which they are parties.

— To make the United Nations more effective in maintaining peace and security by giving it the resources and tools it needs for conflict prevention, peaceful resolution of disputes, peacekeeping, post-conflict peace-building and reconstruction. In this context, we take note of the report of the Panel on United Nations Peace Operations and request the General Assembly to consider its recommendations expeditiously.

— To strengthen cooperation between the United Nations and regional organizations, in accordance with the provisions of Chapter VIII of the Charter.

— To ensure the implementation, by States Parties, of treaties in areas such as arms control and disarmament and of international humanitarian law and human rights law, and call upon all States to consider signing and ratifying the Rome Statute of the International Criminal Court.

— To take concerted action against international terrorism, and to accede as soon as possible to all the relevant international conventions.

— To redouble our efforts to implement our commitment to counter the world drug problem.

— To intensify our efforts to fight transnational crime in all its dimensions, including trafficking as well as smuggling in human beings and money laundering.

— To minimize the adverse effects of United Nations economic sanctions on innocent populations, to subject such sanctions regimes to regular reviews and to eliminate the adverse effects of sanctions on third parties.

— To strive for the elimination of weapons of mass destruction, particularly nuclear weapons, and to keep all options open for achieving this aim, including the possibility of convening an international conference to identify ways of eliminating nuclear dangers.

— To take concerted action to end illicit traffic in small arms and light weapons, especially by making arms transfers more transparent and supporting regional disarmament measures, taking account of all the recommendations of the forthcoming United Nations Conference on Illicit Trade in Small Arms and Light Weapons.

— To call on all States to consider acceding to the Convention on the Prohibition of the Use, Stockpiling, Production and Transfer of Anti-personnel Mines and on Their Destruction, as well as the amended mines protocol to the Convention on conventional weapons.

10. We urge Member States to observe the Olympic Truce, individually and collectively, now and in the future, and to support the International Olympic Committee in its efforts to promote peace and human understanding through sport and the Olympic Ideal.

III. Development and poverty eradication

11. We will spare no effort to free our fellow men,

women and children from the abject and dehumanizing conditions of extreme poverty, to which more than a billion of them are currently subjected. We are committed to making the right to development a reality for everyone and to freeing the entire human race from want.

12. We resolve therefore to create an environment - at the national and global levels alike - which is conducive to development and to the elimination of poverty.

13. Success in meeting these objectives depends, inter alia, on good governance within each country. It also depends on good governance at the international level and on transparency in the financial, monetary and trading systems. We are committed to an open, equitable, rule-based, predictable and non-discriminatory multilateral trading and financial system.

14. We are concerned about the obstacles developing countries face in mobilizing the resources needed to finance their sustained development. We will therefore make every effort to ensure the success of the High-level International and Intergovernmental Event on Financing for Development, to be held in 2001.

15. We also undertake to address the special needs of the least developed countries. In this context, we welcome the Third United Nations Conference on the Least Developed Countries to be held in May 2001 and will endeavour to ensure its success. We call on the industrialized countries:

— To adopt, preferably by the time of that Conference, a policy of duty- and quota-free access for essentially all exports from the least developed countries;

— To implement the enhanced programme of debt relief for the heavily indebted poor countries without further delay and to agree to cancel all official bilateral debts of those countries in return for their making demonstrable commitments to poverty reduction; and

— To grant more generous development assistance, especially to countries that are genuinely making an effort to apply their resources to poverty reduction.

16. We are also determined to deal comprehensively and effectively with the debt problems of low- and middle-income developing countries, through various national and international measures designed to make their debt sustainable in the long term.

17. We also resolve to address the special needs of small island developing States, by implementing the Barbados Programme of Action and the outcome of the twenty-second special session of the General Assembly rapidly and in full. We urge the international community to ensure that, in the development of a vulnerability index, the special needs of small island developing States are taken into account.

18. We recognize the special needs and problems of the landlocked developing countries, and urge both bilateral and multilateral donors to increase financial and technical assistance to this group of countries :o

meet their special development needs and to help them overcome the impediments of geography by improving their transit transport systems.

19. We resolve further:

— To halve, by the year 2015, the proportion of the world's people whose income is less than one dollar a day and the proportion of people who suffer from hunger and, by the same date, to halve the proportion of people who are unable to reach or to afford safe drinking water.

— To ensure that, by the same date, children everywhere, boys and girls alike, will be able to complete a full course of primary schooling and that girls and boys will have equal access to all levels of education.

— By the same date, to have reduced maternal mortality by three quarters, and under-five child mortality by two thirds, of their current rates.

— To have, by then, halted, and begun to reverse, the spread of HIV/AIDS, the scourge of malaria and other major diseases that afflict humanity.

— To provide special assistance to children orphaned by HIV/AIDS.

— By 2020, to have achieved a significant improvement in the lives of at least 100 million slum dwellers as proposed in the "Cities Without Slums" initiative.

20. We also resolve:

— To promote gender equality and the empowerment of women as effective ways to combat poverty, hunger and disease and to stimulate development that is truly sustainable.

— To develop and implement strategies that give young people everywhere a real chance to find decent and productive work.

— To encourage the pharmaceutical industry to make essential drugs more widely available and affordable by all who need them in developing countries.

— To develop strong partnerships with the private sector and with civil society organizations in pursuit of development and poverty eradication.

— To ensure that the benefits of new technologies, especially information and communication technologies, in conformity with recommendations contained in the ECOSOC 2000 Ministerial Declaration, are available to all.

IV. Protecting our common environment

21. We must spare no effort to free all of humanity, and above all our children and grandchildren, from the threat of living on a planet irredeemably spoilt by human activities, and whose resources would no longer be sufficient for their needs.

22. We reaffirm our support for the principles of sustainable development, including those set out in Agenda 21, agreed upon at the United Nations Conference on Environment and Development.

23. We resolve therefore to adopt in all our environmental actions a new ethic of conservation and stewardship and, as first steps, we resolve:

— To make every effort to ensure the entry into force of the Kyoto Protocol, preferably by the tenth anniversary of the United Nations Conference on Environment and Development in 2002, and to embark on the required reduction in emissions of greenhouse gases.

— To intensify our collective efforts for the management, conservation and sustainable development of all types of forests.

— To press for the full implementation of the Convention on Biological Diversity and the Convention to Combat Desertification in those Countries Experiencing Serious Drought and/or Desertification, particularly in Africa.

— To stop the unsustainable exploitation of water resources by developing water management strategies at the regional, national and local levels, which promote both equitable access and adequate supplies.

— To intensify cooperation to reduce the number and effects of natural and man-made disasters.

— To ensure free access to information on the human genome sequence.

V. Human rights, democracy and good governance

24. We will spare no effort to promote democracy and strengthen the rule of law, as well as respect for all internationally recognized human rights and fundamental freedoms, including the right to development.

25. We resolve therefore:

- To respect fully and uphold the Universal Declaration of Human Rights.
- To strive for the full protection and promotion in all our countries of civil, political, economic, social and cultural rights for all.
- To strengthen the capacity of all our countries to implement the principles and practices of democracy and respect for human rights, including minority rights.
- To combat all forms of violence against women and to implement the Convention on the Elimination of All Forms of Discrimination against Women.
- To take measures to ensure respect for and protection of the human rights of migrants, migrant workers and their families, to eliminate the increasing acts of racism and xenophobia in many societies and to promote greater harmony and tolerance in all societies.
- To work collectively for more inclusive political processes, allowing genuine participation by all citizens in all our countries.
- To ensure the freedom of the media to perform their essential role and the right of the public to have access to information.

VI. Protecting the vulnerable

26. We will spare no effort to ensure that children and all civilian populations that suffer disproportionately the consequences of natural disasters, genocide, armed

conflicts and other humanitarian emergencies are given every assistance and protection so that they can resume normal life as soon as possible. We resolve therefore:

— To expand and strengthen the protection of civilians in complex emergencies, in conformity with international humanitarian law.

— To strengthen international cooperation, including burden sharing in, and the coordination of humanitarian assistance to, countries hosting refugees and to help all refugees and displaced persons to return voluntarily to their homes, in safety and dignity and to be smoothly reintegrated into their societies.

— To encourage the ratification and full implementation of the Convention on the Rights of the Child and its optional protocols on the involvement of children in armed conflict and on the sale of children, child prostitution and child pornography.

VII. Meeting the special needs of Africa

27. We will support the consolidation of democracy in Africa and assist Africans in their struggle for lasting peace, poverty eradication and sustainable development, thereby bringing Africa into the mainstream of the world economy.

28. We resolve therefore:

— To give full support to the political and institutional structures of emerging democracies in Africa.

— To encourage and sustain regional and subregional mechanisms for preventing conflict and promoting political stability, and to ensure a reliable flow of resources for peacekeeping operations on the continent.

— To take special measures to address the challenges of poverty eradication and sustainable development in Africa, including debt cancellation, improved market access, enhanced Official Development Assistance and increased flows of Foreign Direct Investment, as well as transfers of technology.

— To help Africa build up its capacity to tackle the spread of the HIV/AIDS pandemic and other infectious diseases.

VIII. Strengthening the United Nations

29. We will spare no effort to make the United Nations a more effective instrument for pursuing all of these priorities: the fight for development for all the peoples of the world, the fight against poverty, ignorance and disease; the fight against injustice; the fight against violence, terror and crime; and the fight against the degradation and destruction of our common home.

30. We resolve therefore:

— To reaffirm the central position of the General Assembly as the chief deliberative, policy-making and representative organ of the United Nations, and to enable it to play that role effectively.

— To intensify our efforts to achieve a comprehensive reform of the Security Council in all its aspects.

— To strengthen further the Economic and Social Council, building on its recent achievements, to help it fulfil the role ascribed to it in the Charter.

— To strengthen the International Court of Justice, in order to ensure justice and the rule of law in international affairs.

— To encourage regular consultations and coordination among the principal organs of the United Nations in pursuit of their functions.

— To ensure that the Organization is provided on a timely and predictable basis with the resources it needs to carry out its mandates.

— To urge the Secretariat to make the best use of those resources, in accordance with clear rules and procedures agreed by the General Assembly, in the interests of all Member States, by adopting the best management practices and technologies available and by concentrating on those tasks that reflect the agreed priorities of Member States.

— To promote adherence to the Convention on the Safety of United Nations and Associated Personnel.

— To ensure greater policy coherence and better cooperation between the United Nations, its agencies, the Bretton Woods Institutions and the World Trade Organization, as well as other multilateral bodies, with a view to achieving a fully coordinated approach to the problems of peace and development.

— To strengthen further cooperation between the United Nations and national parliaments through their world organization, the Inter-Parliamentary Union, in various fields, including peace and security, economic and social development, international law and human rights and democracy and gender issues.

— To give greater opportunities to the private sector, non-governmental organizations and civil society, in general, to contribute to the realization of the Organization's goals and programmes.

31. We request the General Assembly to review on a regular basis the progress made in implementing the provisions of this Declaration, and ask the Secretary-General to issue periodic reports for consideration by the General Assembly and as a basis for further action.

32. We solemnly reaffirm, on this historic occasion, that the United Nations is the indispensable common house of the entire human family, through which we will seek to realize our universal aspirations for peace, cooperation and development. We therefore pledge our unstinting support for these common objectives and our determination to achieve them.

Bibliography

Abrams, Alan (1997), *Diversity and the Internet, Journal of Commerce*, June 26.

Anderson, Teresa E. and Alan Melchior (1995), *Assessing Telecommunications Technology as a Tool for Urban Community Building*, Journal of Urban Technology, Vol. 3, No 1, 29-44.

Coley, Richard J., Cradler, John, and Engel, Penelope K. (1997), *Computers and Classrooms: The Status of Technology in U.S. Schools, ETS Policy Information Report*. ETS Policy Information Center.

Harmon, Amy (1997), *Net Day Volunteers Back to Wire Schools for Internet*, New York Times, October 25.

Hoffman, D.L. and T.P. Novak (1996), *Marketing in Hypermedia Computer-Mediated Environments: Conceptual Foundations*, Journal of Marketing, 60 (July), 50-68.

Hoffman, D.L., W.D. Kalsbeek and T.P. Novak (1996), *Internet and Web Use in the United States: Baselines for Commercial Development, Special Section on Internet in the Home, Communications of the ACM*, 39 (December).

Hoffman, Donna L., Thomas P. Novak and Alladi Venkatesh (1997), *Diversity on the Internet: The Relationship of Race to Access and Usage*, Paper presented at the Aspen Institute's Forum on Diversity and the Media , Queenstown, Maryland, November 5-7, 1997.

Holmes, Tamara E. (1997), *Seeing a Future With More Blacks Exploring the Internet*, USA Today, February 20.

Katz, James and Philip Aspden (1997), *Motivations for and Barriers to Internet Usage: Results of a National Public Opinion Survey*, Paper presented at the 24th Annual Telecommunications Policy Research Conference, Solomons, Maryland, October 6, 1996.

Keller, James (1996), *Public Access Issues: An Introduction.*

Kelly T: *IP connectivity in the Least Developed Countries*; ITU April 2002

Kirkman Geoffrey S.: *Out of the Labs and Into the Developing World: Using Appropriate Technologies to Promote Truly Global Internet Diffusion*, Center for International Development at Harvard University, March 2001.

Lawrence, Steve and C. Lee Giles, (1998), *Searching the World Wide Web, Science*, Volume 280, Number 5360, p. 98. Network Wizards (1998), Internet Domain Survey, July.

Nielsen Media Research (1997), *The Spring 1997 CommerceNet/ Nielsen Media Internet Demographic Survey*, Full Report, Volume I of II.

Princeton, NJ. CyberAtlas (1998), *Demographics: Who's on the Net in the US?*

Rutkowski, Anthony M. (1998), *Internet Trends*, February. Center for Next Generation Internet, Washington, D.C.

UNCTAD (2001) ; *Report on electronic trade and development ; United Nations publications*, Geneva

UNESCO (1999-2000) *World report on communication and information*

Index